A Consumer's Guide to Preaching

A Consumer's Guide to Preaching

JAY ADAMS

VICTOR BOOKS®

A DIVISION OF SCRIPTURE PRESS PUBLICATIONS INC.
USA CANADA ENGLAND

Unless otherwise noted, Scripture quotations are from *The Christian Counselor's New Testament* by Jay E. Adams, © 1977 by Presbyterian and Reformed Publishing Company. Other quotations are from *The Modern Language Bible: The Berkeley Version in Modern English* (MCB), © 1945, 1959, 1969 by Zondervan Publishing House, used by permission.

Library of Congress Cataloging-in-Publication Data

Adams, Jay Edward.
  A consumer's guide to preaching / by Jam Adams.
    p.   cm.
  Includes bibliographical references.
  ISBN 0-89693-398-9
  1. Preaching. 2. Listening—Religious aspects—Christianity. 3. Word of God (Theology) 4. Christian life—1960–   I. Title.
  BV4235.L57A32   1991   90-27751
  251—dc20   CIP

---

1 2 3 4 5 6 7 8 9 10 Printing/Year 95 94 93 92 91

Contents

Preface

Chapter 1 There Is a Problem **11**

Chapter 2 Before You Begin **17**

Chapter 3 Preparing for Preaching **23**

Chapter 4 Your Basic Attitude **31**

Chapter 5 Expectations, Predisposition,
and Spiritual State **39**

Chapter 6 Work at Getting the
Message **47**

Chapter 7 Understanding the
Message **57**

Chapter 8 How to Handle Poor
Preaching **65**

Chapter 9 Berean Listening **73**

Chapter 10 Distractions **81**

Chapter 11 The Preacher and You **89**

Chapter 12 Implementation **97**

Chapter 13 God, Your Neighbor, and
        You **105**

Chapter 14 Technical Matters **113**

Chapter 15 Conclusion **121**

Chapter 16 Sermon Slices **125**

Notes **157**

Preface

"What's wrong with preaching?"

Why don't preachers learn their craft more thoroughly?"

"Most preaching is boring."

"I hardly ever get fed at church."

"I don't get anything out of my preacher's sermons."

"From the minute he reads the text, I know what he's going to say."

"These—and dozens of complaints like them—may be heard in many gatherings of Bible-believing Christians talking seriously about their church. What's the problem? Why is there so much dissatisfaction with preaching? Is it legitimate? And, if so, can anything be done about it?

Granted, there are thousands of inept preachers. Granted, many theological seminaries do a far-less-than-adequate job of training them. Granted, many ministers—perhaps even a majority—do not belong in the ministry. Granting all this, I still say in such talk, more often than not, preachers get a bum rap!

Too many laymen speak about the preaching event as if it were a one-way street, as if the responsibility for what transpires when the Bible is proclaimed rests solely on the shoulders of the preacher. But that's not so! Effective communication demands competence from all parties.

Preaching is not like sculpture, automotive mechanics, or toy manufacturing. The preacher must work with people who doze, resist, misunderstand, and easily become angry. The task of communicating God's message, therefore, is not simple. Unlike clay, metal, and plastic, the listener plays an active role in the communication process—for good or ill.

As a matter of fact, not only does the listener have a role to play in the momentous occasion on which God speaks to His people through the mouth of a preacher delivering His Word, but the Scriptures themselves say more about the listener's responsibility to hear, understand, and implement the message than about the preacher's obligation to faithfully preach it. That's why I say to dump all the blame on the preacher is a bum rap.

And, when you compare the amount of bad press preaching gets (much of it is warranted, I'll grant you), the number of books written (I have over 300 in my own library), courses taught (you can even earn a doctorate in preaching) and work done to improve preaching (all necessary, of course) with the virtual absence of comment, courses, or training materials having to do with listening, again, I say, preachers are getting a bum rap!

It is time to cross to the other side of this two-way street. It is time to speak plainly, frankly, and helpfully to consumers of preaching. It is time for those who are so ready to complain to humbly admit their own deficiencies in listening. Certainly, too, many already recognize their failures and would welcome practical, biblical advice about how to get more out of preaching. But they simply don't know what to do to improve listening skills. In either case, something must be done to bring balance into this altogether lopsided situation.

Now it is not mainly about fairness that I am concerned—please don't construe my words as a defense of sloppy preaching—I want to see more effective communication taking place as the result of responsible, joint activity on both sides. I have devoted most of my ministry to helping preachers become more effective communicators. But, over the years, I have become more and more convinced that such efforts alone will not solve the problem. Listeners need training too. That's why I wrote this book.

I have ransacked the BR-BX sections of libraries in several Christian institutions, looking through volumes on Christian living, spiritual growth, sermons, etc., trying to find what others have said about listening to sermons. There is virtually nothing but scraps—a passing comment here, an illustration there. Writers purporting to tell Christians how to grow spiritually and serve well, apparently consider the preaching of the Word and one's response to it, unimportant to the process. Or, perhaps, this flagrant omission represents their own disillusionment with preaching.

That attitude is contrary to what the Reformers, who put so much stock in preaching, thought and it also opposes what New Testament writers taught. The attitude probably accounts for much of the laxity (and, often downright flippancy) regarding preaching today.

It is my contention that one reason why people are not growing as they should is that instead of encouraging Christians to drink deeply of the Word, as preached, preachers set their flock on a course of pseudo self-sufficiency that often deceives them into thinking they are sufficient interpreters of Scripture, when they are not. This kind of thinking makes believers critics of preaching rather than listeners and learners, and that confuses people about the true place of Bible study and the priesthood of all believers.

I have written this book because of the dearth of material devoted to genuine concern for preaching from the listener's point of view. So far as I know, there is no other book like it.

I do not wish to promote a new prelacy—a one-man show—that ignores the ministry of laypersons spelled out in Ephesians 4:12. Indeed, as you will discover, I believe the layperson has a far greater role to play than that emphasized in most books. Most books on the Christian life fail to emphasize preaching as a principal means by which the Holy Spirit promotes spiritual growth. While stressing Ephesians 4:12, one must never forget Ephesians 4:11! What I am after is biblical balance—balance that recognizes, on the one hand, that preaching alone will not do the trick, but on the other hand, stresses that preaching is seriously deficient apart from lay study. What this book calls for then, is a joint venture. And, it endeavors to spell that out in concrete terms which any intelligent layperson may understand and follow.

In your hands is a volume designed to help you get the most out of any sermon. I am sure that most complaints about preaching (rather than congregations) can be put to sleep, if only you, and thousands of other Christians like you, become concerned enough to take the time and expend the effort necessary to become proficient listeners. It is not only effective preaching that we need; we also need congregations that know how to listen, understand, and implement God's truth.

In the pages that follow I shall introduce you to some of the numerous biblical injunctions that delineate the listener's responsibility. I shall confront and offer solutions to many problems encountered in listening to sermons, and I shall outline a program for helping sincere churchgoers sharpen their communication skills.

"Can you tell me what to do when I have to listen to sermons that are frequently dull, sometimes puerile, and often inane? If not, I see no use in reading further. That's what I confront almost every week. And, it's no use telling me to change churches. That won't do—there aren't any other evangelical churches in our small town. I'm stuck!"

Yes, I am even going to tell you what to do when you must listen to inadequate preaching. Be patient; read on. This book is for you too. But, in short, the book is mainly a guide to help the average listener get the most out of preaching—whatever it may be like.

CHAPTER ONE

There Is a Problem

You may have readily identified with one or more of the sample complaints in the Preface to this book. Those complaints highlight a serious problem in the church. No one, so far as I know, pretends that the problem is new, but it seems that modern conditions underscore and aggravate it as never before.

In many, possibly most, congregations today thoughtful people are disturbed about what they perceive to be a problem with preaching. Not only does this perception take many forms, but it is also variously expressed. Yet, as we strip away verbiage and other secondary factors, increasingly, what we find concerned Christians saying is: "I just don't get much out of preaching." And every indication seems to confirm the fact—Christians are *not* getting what they should from the sermon.

Certainly, many factors contribute to this sad situation. Some preachers speak poorly. Others spend far too little time preparing their messages. Still others, anxious to provide "meat" for their people, spend all week doing exegetical shopping, only to serve their congregations fine cuts of meat as bloody, uncooked slabs fit only for tigers. Many preachers follow the impersonal lecture-method taught by most homileticians and speak *about* the Bible rather than about God and the needs of the congregation *from* the Bible. They are content to squeeze the juice from a passage, and then fling into the pews the dry, abstract husk that is left. All these—and numerous other failings—characterize much contemporary preaching.

These problems and others like them are an important part

(but only a *part*) of the larger problem mentioned above. Christians are *not* getting much out of preaching, but the problem isn't only in the pulpit, it is also in the pew. And yet, nothing is being done about it.

Nowhere today can you find information—books, courses, or otherwise—about how to listen to a sermon so as to get the most out of it. Indeed, no one seems to be concerned about training Christians in the fine, but difficult, art of listening. The false assumption is that if only a preacher would do his job well enough, effective communication would take place. That assumption, along with all that is built on it, is the fundamental error that, every bit as much as poor preaching itself, has led to the sorry plight of the church today. People by the hundreds of thousands attend church every week but carry so little away. Their lives suffer, their homes show it, and the meager impact they make for Christ is clear evidence that very little is happening. Preaching, even good preaching, is not doing the job.

Hearing—An Ethical Issue
But, as I have been saying, sermonic ineffectiveness is not only the fault of preachers; listeners must share the blame. I have made whatever contribution I can to preaching through numerous volumes designed to help preachers do a better job.[1] Now, I want to address the other half of the problem: listening.

When Jesus says, "Whoever has ears, let him hear" (Matt. 13:9) and repeats the same expression at the conclusion to each of the letters to the seven churches in Revelation (chapters 2–3), He thereby strongly indicates that He expects His people to pay attention to what He says. Indeed, the expression seems to be one of His favorites. In the same passage in Matthew, He sets forth the law of listening:

> Whoever has will be given more, and he will have more than he needs, but whoever doesn't have it, even what he does have will be taken away (Matt. 13:12).

Jesus then speaks of some who, in accordance with Isaiah's prophecy, "hear," yet don't really hear because they don't understand (Matt. 13:13-15). But, in the same breath, He assures the disciples that they are "blessed" because they do hear (v. 16).

Jesus continues the theme, telling the Parable of the Sower, in which there are those who "hear" but do not understand, those who "hear" but the message is choked before it can produce any fruit (13:19-22). These three descriptions of faulty hearing portray a kind of hearing that is not only unprofitable, but also condemned. And, of greatest importance, you will notice that it is the character of the soil, not the sower, that makes all the difference. Jesus also mentions that those who understand the message are affected by it and bear fruit of varying quantities (13:13). Then, after explaining the Parable of the Weeds, He concludes this important discourse by repeating, "Whoever has ears, let him hear."

In the parallel passage in Mark 4:24, after explaining the parables, the author makes this important addition: "Be careful about what you hear." And Luke appends the same parable with these significant words: "So then, be careful how you listen" (Luke 8:18).

These strong words about listening, you will note, are aimed not at the preacher but at those who listen to him. Again and again, in all sorts of forms, the command goes forth from God's Word: "Listen; listen carefully, so that your life may be affected by what you hear and the message will cause you to become fruitful."

But that is not all. At the conclusion of the Sermon on the Mount, the point of the motivational parable of the two foundations is not, as some suppose, to trust Christ as Saviour (however important that may be), but to *hear* and *obey* His words (Matt. 7:24). Again, in this parable, we are warned of the destruction and ruin for the one who "hears these words . . . and doesn't do them" (Matt. 7:26).

"But, that has to do with listening to Christ; not to some modern preacher," you say.

Yes, but be careful about that sort of thinking. Listen to what the Lord Himself said, "Whoever hears you hears Me, and whoever rejects you rejects Me" (Luke 10:16). Hearing preachers who preach His Word, *is* hearing Christ; rejecting preachers who preach His Word *is* rejecting Christ. "How can they hear without a preacher?" (Rom. 10:14)[2]

How All Our Problems Began

Why is listening to preaching so important? Because God speaks by His Word. To fail to hear and heed what He says is an insult. It was just such an insult that plunged the human race into sin and misery. God spoke; Satan spoke. Adam ignored God's Word and listened to Satan instead. The issue, from Eden on, has always been whether people will listen to God or someone else. In the end, regardless of who else speaks, the choice is always the same: God or Satan. Often people fail to hear God because their ears are filled with other words. People will listen—but, to whom? That is the question.

When people listen to God in repentance, faith, and obedience, God pours out His blessings on them. When they ignore God's Word in favor of the counsel of the ungodly, and treat it lightly, He sends a curse. In the Garden, preaching was not the problem; the problem had to do with listening! And that has been a major difficulty ever since: people will hear someone else rather than God.

Like disobedient children, people do not want to listen. Even believers, habituated in ways of disobedience, have great difficulty listening to God. Perhaps from these considerations, you begin to see how important listening is. Through Isaiah, God explained it this way to His backsliding people: "My thoughts are not your thoughts, neither are your ways My ways" (Isa. 55:9). Because of this, people all the more need to listen to God. Otherwise, they will go astray following their own thoughts into their own ways. God calls on you to forsake your thoughts and ways (Isa. 55:7) and listen to His Word (vv. 10-11) so that you may be able to think His thoughts after Him and walk in His steps. And, He insists that His Word never goes forth pointlessly but always accomplishes that for which He sent it. To those with hearing ears, His Word is the sweet sound of blessing; to those who stop their ears, it is the rumble of not-so-distant wrath. The Word of the Lord is always effective—it either softens or hardens hearts. The responsibility to receive it in faith for blessing rests on all who hear. As a listener, you must do some things that a preacher cannot do for you.

All too often today, as in the Garden of Eden, people refuse to listen, counting the preaching of the Word "foolishness," but to those who believe, it is the saving power of God (1 Cor. 1:18).

When God wants to get His people's attention, He shouts "Hear, O Israel" (Deut. 5:1; 6:4; 9:1). The Father stresses that acceptable hearing leads to obedience (Deut. 6:3; 15:5). When people refused to listen to Him, God declared He would refuse to listen to them (Deut. 1:43-45). When they found themselves in trouble because of their sin, He commanded them to "turn" (repent) and "listen" (Deut. 4:30). And so it goes throughout the entire Bible, in book after book, chapter after chapter, God calls on people to listen. Hearing is a dominant theme of both Old and New Testaments—far more dominant than the duty of preachers to proclaim the Word.

Why, then, has the duty of listening been overlooked? I am sure such negligence involves many factors. But let me mention one. At the outset, when God confronted Adam and Eve about failing to listen to Him, they did not acknowledge their sin as such but, instead, tried to excuse themselves by shifting the blame. Adam said, "The woman You gave me. . . ." Eve's reply was, "The serpent. . . ." Neither sought God's forgiveness for listening to Satan rather than to God. Similarly, ever since, it has been easier for sinners to blame preachers than to admit their own reluctance to listen. Harry Ironside was not very far from stating the truth when he quipped that although he had the gift of preaching, not every congregation had the gift of hearing. Closer to the truth is that fact that all true congregations have the gift, but it is often poorly developed and wrongly used.

CHAPTER TWO

Before You Begin

W ell, if preaching is as important as God says, and I put myself in jeopardy if I treat it lightly, despise, or neglect it, then I suppose I'd better get serious about learning to listen. But what must I do? How do I go about improving my listening skills? What is involved in 'getting the most out of a sermon'? I don't even know where to begin!"

Good questions—all of which I propose to answer in time. If your heart is right and you are anxious to learn, you should make great strides quickly. But first let's consider that *"if"* in the last sentence.

The Absolute Prerequisite

For years, his wife dragged him to church. Every Sunday morning, it was the same old routine:

"Bill, aren't you ever going to get up? You'll be late for church."

"Aw, Mary, go without me. I'm tired. It's more comfortable sleeping here than in a pew."

"No way. Get out of that bed and get dressed. And while we're at it, tell me, why don't you pay attention to what Pastor Murgatroyd has to say? He's not a bad preacher."

"Oh? You could have fooled me! Frankly, I'd have to take Nodoze to stay awake during one of his sermons."

One Sunday, Bill was up before Mary. He had showered, shaved, and dressed long before she crawled from between the sheets. He couldn't wait to get to church. He was looking forward to hearing the next in a series of sermons that the pastor had begun two weeks ago. What happened? Had Pastor Murgatroyd taken a refresher course in preaching? Had he changed his style of preaching? Was the subject matter so much different? No. Something else had taken place. Bill had changed.

All progress in the Christian life, including learning to get the most out of preaching has one absolute precondition. You can't grow as a Christian until you become one! What made the difference in Bill is that he became a Christian.

Becoming a Christian is not like joining a club or taking a new job. It involves more than an outer change of circumstances. You become a Christian only through an inner change so radical that the Bible refers to it as a new birth. And, it is radical enough to create interest in the preaching of the Scriptures where previously there was none.

Apart from such a change, listening to preaching will be, at best, unprofitable. It will bore, enrage, confuse, or turn you off—even when the preaching itself is good. Do you find that's true for you?

People—all people—are born sinners, estranged from God, and therefore, unwilling and unable to welcome His Word. As Paul put it:

> A natural person doesn't welcome the teachings of God's Spirit; they are foolishness to him, and he isn't able to know about them because they must be investigated spiritually (1 Cor. 2:14).

In the same chapter Paul explained the difference between a "natural" person and a "spiritual" person. Everyone is born with a sinfully-oriented nature, inherited from his parents Naturally, he begins to live life according to that nature. Because he comes into life antagonistic to God's truth, he has no "natural" interest in preaching. Indeed, if anything, he is turned off by it. That is why the average person will have little or nothing to do with serious, biblical preaching, though for social or business advantage he may often attend church and even make a spurious profession of faith. In such cases, he may hold his basic antagonism in check so that it does not show. Yet, all the while, he remains a "natural" person, far from God and adverse to His Word. Nothing supernatural has happened to change him.

If, for some reason, a "natural" person, basically oriented wrongly toward the Scriptures, attempts to understand a passage from the Bible, he finds it hard going. He wonders why Christians become so interested in studying the Bible; to him it is dull and uninteresting, and in most places simply doesn't make sense. No wonder the Bills of this world want to stay in bed rather than listen to Pastor Murgatroyd!

The principle involved holds true in all areas of life: prejudice (or some other negative orientation) always hinders communication. Turner, the painter, got a reputation for refusing to give advice to young, aspiring artists not because he didn't want to, but because he found that so many of them were in no state of mind to accept his advice. If this principle is true of matters so inconsequential, how much more must it be true of matters of eternal consequence! The play may be a success but the audience a failure.

It is possible that I have been describing your condition. Indeed, all of us were born with a sinful nature that naturally turns from God and His Word. Unless, therefore, you have been transformed by God's grace, you are still in your sins, alienated from the truth of God. There is no way for you to benefit from preaching unless you trust in Jesus Christ as Saviour, believing the Good News of His redeeming death and resurrection.

In order to get what you should from preaching you must become a *spiritual* person. The word *spiritual* has nothing to do with grades or stages of Christian growth as some suppose. All Christians are *spiritual* or they are not Christians. By definition, a Christian is one who has the Spirit: "If anyone doesn't have Christ's Spirit, he isn't His" (Rom. 8:9). When God transforms a person and gives him new life, He does so by placing the Holy Spirit within, thus making him a *spiritual* person. His life is now Spirit-motivated and God-oriented.

What the eye hasn't seen and *the ear hasn't heard,* and
what hasn't been conceived by the human heart, is what
God has prepared for those who love Him. To us God
revealed it by His Spirit. . . . the spiritual person is able
to investigate everything . . . we have the mind of Christ
(1 Cor. 2:9, 10, 15, 16).

That is what happened to Bill. And it can happen to you.

In the room where you are sitting there are sights and
sounds all around that you cannot see or hear unless you
have your television turned on. That's much the way it is
with the natural person: he can neither see nor hear God's
truth *as truth* without the receiving set. God's Spirit is like
the TV. When He enters a person, He changes his life direction and gives him a new capability to see all of life different-
ly. He enables him to listen to God for the first time. His life
is radically reoriented. From the moment he trusts Christ as
Saviour, he is able to enjoy preaching for what it is: God's
message of blessing to him. Indeed, one of the earliest evi-
dences of true conversion is hunger for the preaching of the
Word.

While that is true, it is also true that the old habits,
thoughts, and ways, developed while in the natural state,
persist. They continue to hinder communication, even when
the Christian desires it.[1] That is why he must actively learn
to replace the old ways with new ways of hearing God. This
book is designed to help you overcome such problems and
teach you how to get more and more out of preaching. But
that must begin with the new birth.

"Where, exactly, *do* I begin?" you ask. Well, if you have
never done so, you must first acknowledge the fact that you
are a sinner. That means that you have broken God's laws
and stand condemned as one who has failed to listen to His
Word. You have lived as though God doesn't exist, as if you
were not responsible to Him, and as if He has done or said
nothing about human responsibility and sin. Of course, that's
untrue. He did the *supreme* thing He could do: He sent His

Son, Jesus Christ, to die on the cross for guilty sinners like you. He gave His Word that those who believe Christ died for them will have all their sins forgiven, the very moment they believe. He sent preachers everywhere to proclaim this Good News. And He sends His Spirit to enable His people to believe by giving them new hearts and *spiritual* life.

Do you believe? Have you been forgiven? Do you have new life? If not, there is no sense reading further until you settle that matter with God. Spiritual life is the *one absolute prerequisite* for profitable listening to preaching.

I urge you to lay all other matters aside until you have come to know the forgiveness of sins and the assurance of eternal life. Nothing is as important as that. In no other way can you honor God and believe and follow what He has to say. Forget preaching and the problems that are connected with it; believe the Good News and be saved. This is the Good News by which Paul said he was saved:

> that Christ died for our sins in agreement with the Scriptures, that He was buried, and that He was raised on the third day, in agreement with the Scriptures (1 Cor. 15:3-4).

On the cross He suffered the punishment for the sins of all who believe, fully paying their penalty. He died in their stead. God raised Him from the dead, not only proclaiming thereby that He accepted Christ's death as a sufficient, substitutionary sacrifice for their sins, but also providing a living Saviour in whom believers may find help in time of need. Will you trust Him now?

If you have trusted Christ as the result of reading this chapter, you should immediately become part of a church that faithfully preaches the Bible. If you are not sure about any given church, you might show this chapter to the pastor. If he agrees with the message taught here, it is likely that you have chosen a church that preaches the Gospel. If you are still not sure or cannot find such a church, kindly write to me in care of the publisher and I will direct you to one.

CHAPTER THREE

Preparing for Preaching

When seed is sown, everything depends on the condition of the ground. That's what the Lord's Word tells us in His Parable of the Soils. The writer of Hebrews put it this way:

> Indeed, the Good News came to us just as it did to them; nevertheless, the word that they heard was of no benefit to them because it wasn't mixed with faith by those who heard it (Heb. 4:2).

That's the sum of it—for the Jews in the wilderness, for the New Testament reader, and for you today. Preaching must be *believed.* To be beneficial, the message must be combined with faith. That is true of salvation, as we saw in the last chapter, and it is true ever after. As a believer goes to hear preaching, he must go ready to mix truth with faith.

But before good seed is sown on good soil, even good soil must be cultivated, and then the crop must be cared for. According to Christ's parable, even the good soil produced varying yields: "some a hundredfold, another sixty and another thirty" (Matt. 13:8). It should be the concern of every Christian to produce a bumper crop. Jesus put it this way: "My Father is glorified by this—that you bear much fruit" (John 15:18). If that is what glorifies God, then, Christian, it is clear that your ambition must be to "bear much fruit."

Preaching is one of God's chief means of sowing seed and helping fruit grow; it is a way of watering and fertilizing the crop. But, you must prepare yourself for the ministry of the Word. You must break up the hard clods that have formed in your soul over the week, turn under the weeds, and prepare the good soil to receive the good seed.

Usually, when we speak of preparation for preaching, we think of the preparation of the preacher. That is important. But in this chapter, we are concerned about the preparation of the listener—a matter of equal importance. Both are essential. If you are not prepared to receive a message, the preacher's preparations will be in vain. How can you prepare yourself to get the most out of preaching? It is important to make a serious effort to do so.

Some Simple Pointers

Sometimes the little things hinder most. Because we think of them as secondary, we treat them as unimportant. Yet, they can be all-important. The evil one loves to capitalize on just such temptations to frustrate good listening.

Getting Adequate Sleep. One of the standard objections to preaching is that "preachers put me to sleep." Usually, the opposite is true: listeners put themselves to sleep. Those who get adequate sleep the night before, rarely go to sleep on Sunday. Jesus was concerned about such simple matters as staying awake. More than once He told His disciples to "watch" (literally, "stay awake" Matt. 24:42; 25:41, etc.). Alertness is important.

Perhaps we have made a great mistake in allowing our time to be ordered by the world. There is good reason to follow the Old Testament method for reckoning time. At creation, it was said that "There was evening and there was morning, one day" (Gen. 1:5, BERK), and so on, throughout the creation week. By this reckoning, a day begins in the evening. The Jews began their Sabbath at sundown. Perhaps, we too should do the same in observing the Lord's Day. Instead of making Saturday night a time to go out, or stay up late watching videos, we might consider it the beginning of the Lord's Day, a time to prepare for worship. It would become a time for the family to relax after the week's activities and go to bed at a respectable hour.

I have caught myself dozing off during a Sunday morning message, even when it was helpful and stimulating and I *wanted* to listen. I can attribute my sleepiness to nothing else but inadequate sleep the night before.

Farmers, construction workers, and others who work outdoors all week are especially vulnerable to the problem. They are used to an abundance of oxygen, and when they find themselves cooped up with others, and a bit short on oxygen, it is easy for them to become drowsy. The phenomenon is similar to the drowsiness caused by a fire in an open fireplace as it consumes oxygen in the process of combustion. Adequate sleep is essential for outdoor workers, then, since they are particularly susceptible to drowsiness in confined quarters where many people are gathered together. A couple of good, stiff cups of coffee for breakfast might also help.

I remember once when I fell asleep preaching—no, not because my sermon was so boring (I knew you'd think that!)—but because I was so tired. For a week I'd been preaching at a church, staying up late every night talking to people, getting up early, visiting all day. I was assigned to a different home every meal—breakfast, lunch, supper, every day. Everyone killed the fatted calf. By Friday night, I was the fatted calf!

During the service that evening, I suddenly awakened to hear myself preaching. I had no idea what I was saying or how to complete the sentence I was well on the way toward ending. It was one of those moments of panic like when you suddenly realize you have dozed off and your car is heading off the road. A horrible experience!

Now, if a preacher can go to sleep preaching—because he is too tired to stay awake—so can you in your more relaxed state, when nothing more is required of you than to listen. Get plenty of sleep; otherwise, count on it—you will be a poor listener.

During a sermon, Bishop Alymer saw that his congregation was inattentive, so he suddenly recited some verses from the Bible in Hebrew. His audience came awake and stared in astonishment. Then, he pointed out the folly of having more interest in an unknown tongue than in the truth they could understand.[1] Does it take something as curious as that to keep you awake during a message?

Getting Ready on Time. One's frame of mind may be set against listening by the hurry and rush of getting to church on time. Blustering in at the last minute after a mad dash through traffic is all it takes to unsettle a family for the remainder of the service.

Now, add to that a battle between husband and wife, parents and children (or all of the above), over someone lagging behind and making the rest late, and you have all the ingredients of a nasty stew. Stewing pew-sitters are poor listeners!

There she sits, wondering what the neighbors must think. Boiling over, her husband had gone out to the car ahead of everyone else, and made his ire known for blocks by honking the horn until the family appeared. *Doesn't he know it takes time to dress the children?* she thinks. *He could lend a hand rather than laying it on the horn!*

He, in turn, sits simmering in the pew, thinking of her tardiness: *Nearly had an accident racing to church after starting so late—then I get an earful about my driving! Hummph! If she can be consistently ten minutes late leaving the house every week, she can be consistently ten minutes earlier—if she wants to.*

Instead of indulging in recrimination, this husband and wife should spend their energies working out a solution. Perhaps they should go to bed earlier, so they could get started earlier the next day. Possibly, they could settle for a lighter breakfast on Sundays, one that takes little time for preparation and consumption; maybe cereal or toast. The husband could help with the kids. The wife could make an effort to be ready *ahead of time.* Little chores, now left till the last minute, could be done on Saturday night. Clothes could be laid out the night before. Older children might even help younger ones get ready.

When you come to church in a relaxed, leisurely way, unconcerned about early morning crises, you will be in a more receptive state of mind.

A Sufficient Breakfast. While some may have to cut down on elaborate breakfasting on Sunday mornings in order to save time, as I said, others may find it beneficial to eat more. Coming to church with an empty or nearly empty stomach can only make you irritable and anxious. You will find yourself sitting there waiting for the service to end so that you can go home and get something to eat. Hungry listeners are poor listeners. Neither irritability nor anxiety is conducive to proper listening. Dieters, in particular, should be careful about this matter. Perhaps they could make Sunday morning breakfast the one meal of the week when dieting is forgotten.

Other Preparations
Studying Ahead. Whenever the pastor announces a series ahead of time, or is preaching through a book of the Bible, you may find it advantageous to do some preliminary study of the passage from which he will preach. Perhaps, in line with a changed perspective on Saturday night such as I discussed above, you will find this night a good time to devote to study.

What should you do? Well, for one thing, you could read over the passage in several translations, noting possible differences that the sermon may clarify. In addition, you may wish to look up the verses in a commentary or two. (A good way to build your library is to buy commentaries in conjunction with sermon series on books of the Bible.)

As you study, make notes of any problems or questions that arise. As you develop this habit, you will soon find yourself concentrating more on your pastor's message. You will be looking for possible connections to your study, and answers to questions study raised. Perhaps the preacher will emphasize something you failed to notice, while (on the other hand) you may have discovered facts he said nothing about. As a result, his message, supplemented by your own study, will yield a richer, fuller understanding of the passage than either the one or the other could alone.

Preparatory study of the passage should also cause you to think of concrete situations to which the verses studied may apply. But, perhaps, you can't quite figure out how. Again, when that happens, you will eagerly listen to the message, hoping to discover the direction that eluded you. And you will soon learn the joy of *participating* rather than merely playing the part of a spectator. If you have always wanted to begin serious Bible study, but don't know how, this might be the very thing that will get you started. More often than not, a good preacher will say something that will clarify the point you have been pondering—even when he doesn't develop a thought as fully as you might wish.

But, in any case—even if he doesn't touch on your particular concerns, looking for such material will make you an alert listener. And, of course, you can always ask your minister later about your interest. Most preachers are delighted when members want to discuss the sermon further—so long as they are truly seeking for understanding.

But you must be careful not to study narrowly, trying to squeeze ideas out of a passage that are not there, then, complaining when the preacher says nothing about your pet interpretations. It is not only preachers who ride hobby horses— you can fall into the same pit. Be careful to accept Scripture for its own concerns. Don't read your concerns into a passage, or force them on your pastor.

When people complain, "I didn't get much out of the sermon," I am tempted to ask, "Well, how much did you bring to it?" You usually get about as much as you anticipate and prepare for.

Prayer. Prayer for the preacher, the congregation, and yourself is important. Time for such prayer might be appropriately found on Saturday night, or whenever it is that you are doing your preparatory study of the verses that will underlie the sermon. Of course, you should also pray for the pastor throughout the week as he is getting material ready to preach.

I shall have more to say about prayer in connection with

preaching later, but for now let me simply remind you of the importance of this matter. Why is it so important? Because what takes place when the Word is preached on Sunday morning and evening is more than a lecture. It is not on a par with a TV documentary. It is unique. It is a time when God speaks to His people from His Word through His appointed herald. In a special way, God is present, working in those who are there. He wants you to ask Him to make His presence profitable to all concerned. Your prayers for your preacher and the rest of the congregation may be what makes the difference between a ho-hum sermon and one that revives the church.

During the Welsh revival of 1859, a preacher was visiting a friend: "I think, Pastor Johnston, the ministers are all *preaching* a great deal better than they used to."

Johnston replied, "Perhaps the people are *hearing* a good deal better than they used to."

"That may be," said the Welsh preacher, "but I think they ought to preach a good deal better."

"Why so?"

"Because the people are all praying now for the ministers."[2]

Doubtless, both men were right. When God blesses in answer to earnest prayer, preachers preach better and listeners listen better. And, the better preachers preach, and listeners listen, the more people will pray. Once begun, the process perpetuates itself.

Regularity. "As was His custom, He went into the synagogue on the Sabbath Day" (Luke 6:16).

Habitual attendance in church is in many ways an aid to listening to the preaching of Scripture. When your participation is spotty, you are likely to feel awkward and apprehensive; conspicuous by your presence. "Will people ask me where I've been? Will they imply as much with their 'Nice to see you, Sally'?" Such self-consciousness can greatly detract from listening.

Moreover, when the minister preaches through a book of

the Bible or on a series of doctrines, irregular attendance hinders listening by breaking continuity. When, for some legitimate reason you cannot attend a sermon in a series, it is wise to obtain a tape and listen to it during the week that follows.

Again, since irregular attendance is disobedience to God (Heb. 10:25) and unless one comes to God with a "true heart . . . full assurance of faith" and a good conscience, he will not approach preaching as he should. If your attendance at the fellowship of believers is inconsistent, you are not likely to "come close to God" (Heb. 10:22) in the spirit He requires. If this has been a problem with you, repent and "do your first works" (Rev. 2:5).

Of course, many other comments could be made about preparing for a sermon, but I do not want you to bite off too much all at once, especially if you are reading along in this book as a part of a group, attempting to implement what you read week by week as you progress. Moreover, I want to speak next about the very important task of preparing *yourself* spiritually so that you will approach the message in a proper attitude. Because of its importance, that matter deserves a separate chapter.

CHAPTER FOUR

Your Basic Attitude

At the conclusion of the last chapter, under the heading of *Regularity*, I said something about the importance of the listener's attitude. In this chapter, I want to enlarge on that matter.

When someone complains, "I didn't get much out of that sermon," I said I often want to reply, "What did you bring to it?" or even more to the point: "What did you bring to put it in?" When you go to the well, it is wise to carry a clean, empty bucket. If you come with a bucket full of bacteria-laden liquid, pour its contents into the well, and then dip out a bucketful, you will get nothing but contaminated water. When you come to church with a mind prejudiced against the preacher, his views, or his preaching as such, no matter what he says or how he says it, you will be sure to find fault. He won't have a chance. You will pour your attitude into the sermon experience, contaminating it from the outset.

What state of mind do you bring to a sermon? Listeners with bad attitudes are poor listeners.

The Right Bias

Of course, we are all biased. There is no way we can totally empty our hearts and minds of bias. Indeed, even if it were possible, it would be undesirable to do so.

As a Christian, you must always be biased toward God—in everything you do. What you need is a *biblical bias*. How can you omit God from your thinking in anything you do? It is precisely by doing so that you fall into error and sin. To glorify God is, in fact, to do all with God in mind, giving Him the honor due Him. If that is true in other things, how much more ought it to be true when you come to meet with Him and listen to His Word?

Regardless of all other factors, you must recognize the preacher for what he is—a herald of God. That is a biblical bias that ought to strongly influence all your thinking toward him. As Paul put it, he is a "man of [*from*] God" (2 Tim. 3:17). You must hold Paul in respect "for his work's sake" (2 Thes. 5:12-13). That means, among other things, you must come positively biased toward his message. How could you do otherwise if you have a biblically-biased attitude toward his office as a herald of God? A herald is one with a message from another. In this case, "from God." The Christian with the proper attitude respects the herald for the office to which he has been called, knowing whom he represents.

"Yes, but what if the herald is a poor preacher?"

I shall devote a chapter to mediocre preaching, and what to do about it, later on. But, for now, in spite of all such considerations, remember whose herald he is. To disrespect him, is to disrespect the One who sent him. Remember, Jesus said:

Whoever hears you hears Me, and whoever rejects you rejects Me. And whoever rejects Me rejects the One who sent Me (Luke 10:16).

Whatever else might be said about the messengers of God, you must surely notice in Christ's words that He closely identifies Himself and the Father with them. To reject the messenger, is to reject God.

Your task, then, is to prepare yourself to receive a message from God—through His accredited messenger. You must approach preaching with a positive bias toward God and the word His messenger brings. What if he *is* a poor preacher? Does that excuse you from listening? Does that give you the right to be a poor listener?

"Well...I guess not," you may say. "But, how can I develop the right attitude?"

To begin with, remind yourself of the facts I have just

mentioned. In addition, remember that you go to church to worship God, a significant part of which worship is to hear what He has to say to you. Certainly, God's Word is more important than the word of any man. If you were listening to a representative of the President of the United States who had come to deliver an important message to you from the President, you would give him your fullest attention. And you would listen attentively to what he had to say—even if the representative himself were most unappealing. After all, a message from the President must not be taken lightly. All your thoughts would be centered on the President, not on his representative. But, what of a message from the Creator of the universe? How much more ought you to give the most careful attention to it, regardless of who delivers it.

It is possible that you might differ with the President on some points; you might even entertain a negative bias toward him. But, even then, you'd probably honor him because of his office, and therefore, honor his representative. The other day, on a Delta flight from Atlanta to LAX, Jimmy Carter boarded and went down the aisles shaking hands with everyone. Even though I strongly differed with much he did as president, I still considered it an honor to shake the hand of a man who had held the office of the President of the United States. Surely, you do not differ with God—unless you are in rebellion against Him. Even then, you should give Him the hearing you would give a formidable and respected enemy!

But, for our purposes, I shall assume you are a Christian, not in outright rebellion against God, but, perhaps, as with most of us, struggling with various sins. In that case, first, and foremost, you must learn to distinguish between the messenger, the message he brings, and the One from whom it springs. Do not construe bias against the messenger as bias against God or His truth. Even if you have something against the preacher (incidentally, you are obligated to straighten this out: Eph. 4:26; Gal. 6:1), you cannot (rightly) have anything against God. Indeed, your respect for God and His Word ought to enhance your respect for His herald—even when, for other reasons, you might have a bias against him.

In "The Sermon and the Lunch," C.S. Lewis tells about a preacher who had been listened to attentively up to the point when he said, "And so, the home life must be the foundation of our national life." Lewis writes:

> And as he spoke I noticed that all confidence in him had departed.... Now the shufflings and coughings began.... The sermon, for all practical purposes, was over—at least for most of us. I was thinking *How can he? How can he of all persons?* I knew the preacher's home pretty well.[1]

Certainly it is hard to avoid such problems. They *do* intrude. But *good* listeners do not allow such matters to get in their way. They look beyond the messenger to the message and, what is of greater import, they look to the One who sent the message.

What the preacher said may be true; indeed Lewis seems to have thought so, or he would not have been so hard on the preacher. As a matter of fact, it may be that the preacher, knowing his own family problems, was trying to warn and help others. Lewis, and the members of the congregation who began coughing and shuffling were poor listeners. It is possible that they missed an important word from God. Their focus was on the preacher and his foibles, not on God.

I am not now speaking of the preacher's responsibility. Of course he is to adorn the Gospel with a life of holiness, and he must do all he can to avoid being an offense (knowing that even C.S. Lewis types can be distracted when he is offensive). But, viewing the matter from the listener's seat, you are responsible to look beyond the messenger to the Lord's message.

An Open Mind?

People talk about an open mind, as if it were possible. Thinking of bias raises questions about your relationship to truth and error. While I shall say more about this later on from a different perspective, here I only want to make the point that you must have an open mind—*toward the Scriptures*. The only way to have an open mind in any proper sense of the term is to be open to *something*. That is what is meant by bias. But Christians are called to choose their biases. From the Garden of Eden, God has set forth two ways (there are not *many* ways, but only two: the narrow way and the broad one; His way and all others). And He calls on us to avoid the tree of the knowledge of good and evil, the curses of Mount Ebal, the unclean ways prohibited by His Law, and the counsel of the ungodly. Instead, He offers us the tree of life, the blessings of Mount Gerazim, the clean ways, and His Law on which to meditate day and night.

An open mind to something, means a closed mind to those things that do not accord with it. Throughout the Scriptures, we find a basic antithesis between God's way and all other ways. He speaks of heaven and hell, the saved and the lost, those who are within and those who are without, truth and error, life and death, light and darkness, righteousness and sin, etc. And He calls on us always to choose the former and reject the latter.

That is bias.

And, that bias means we should approach all things with a desire to choose God's way and reject any other. Indeed, the early church went under the name *The Way* because among all the other options that were offered by men, God interposed the one and only true way of life (See John 14:6; Acts 4:12). This antithetical bias, in which we are called to acknowledge and honor God in all things, is what leads to both a closed and open mind. The Christian's mind ought to be fully open to whatever God says, and all that is consistent with it; but it must be equally as closed to all else.

That is why the proper attitude toward the preaching of the Word must be "I want to learn everything God is saying to me." It is true that the messenger may contaminate the divine message to a greater or lesser extent, and that poses a problem to be considered in a later chapter. But, here I am concerned with the matter of attitude. What is your attitude? Do you, like some, listen in order to detect flaws in the message, or do you listen to discover truth? Do you miss truth because you are so busy detecting error? You must not approach preaching that way. It is a matter of direction. What is your focus—finding fault or learning truth?

"Well," you say, "if you don't know what is error, you will have a hard time discovering truth." Granted. But let me just say this. Bank tellers are not taught how to detect counterfeit money. They focus on the real stuff. By handling the real thing, they learn to detect the false. In much the same way, when you are anxious to obtain all you can from God, you cultivate an attitude that expectantly seeks more truth: "Buy the truth and don't sell it" (Prov. 23:23).

It is a matter of your basic orientation. Fundamentally, you are more interested in truth or error. Subtly, many who claim to be high on truth, turn out to be high on error. Under the guise of truth-seekers, in reality, they are no more than error-detectors. The true Christian attitude, epitomized by the verses that follow, causes one to hunger and thirst for more and more of God's truth:

I am Yours, save me; I have sought Your precepts (Ps. 119:96).

I am Your servant. Give me understanding, that I may know Your testimonies (Ps. 119:125).

I rejoice at Your Word as one who finds great beauty (Ps. 119:162).

Truly, I yearn for Your precepts; give me life according to Your righteousness (Ps. 119:40).

Open my eyes that I may contemplate the wonders of Your Law (Ps. 119:18).

With a focus on the discovery of truth rather than the detection of error, the psalmist could not help but declare: "Through Your precepts I gain discernment; therefore I hate every false way" (Ps. 119:104). That is the proper order. Abhorrence of falsehood in thought and life should flow naturally from delight in the Truth. When He "opened their minds," Luke says, Jesus opened them "to understand the Scriptures" (Luke 24:45). The "openings" mentioned in Luke 24:31-32, 45, all have to do with Scripture. When Christ opens people's minds to God's Word, they see Him "in all the Scriptures" (24:27) and their "hearts burn within" (24:32)! Ask the Holy Spirit to open your mind in a similar way.

The Christian, then, must cultivate a mind that is open to God's truth but closed to error, just as surely as the unbeliever's mind is open to error and closed to the truth. All minds are open to some things and closed to others. It is a matter of choice and cultivation. How do you approach preaching? To what is your mind open?

Expectations, Predisposition, and Spiritual State

Knowledge and learning are not amoral. To suppose so is one of the great errors of modern thought. Even believers are confused about this matter. Christian educators rarely ask questions about the educability of the regenerate against the unregenerate or the Christian walking with God against the one who is out of fellowship with Him.[1] Educators simply assume, given equal gray matter, all are equally educable. They are not. Jesus once said, "Whoever is from God listens to the words that are from God. The reason why you don't listen to them is that you aren't from God" (John 8:47; see also v. 43 and 1 John 4:6).

Learning is a moral-spiritual matter. The Holy Spirit is involved in communicating truth. He enables you to "welcome" it and assimilate it into daily life, as we saw in chapter 2. But it is also true that a Christian out of fellowship with God simply is not in a state of mind to receive or act upon truth. He must first repent of the sin that stands between God and himself.

God is not a cosmic vending machine from whom we may mechanically obtain what we want when we want it by pressing the right buttons. He is a Person. We must be in proper relationship to Him in order to benefit from His Word. Writing to Christians, James says:

But let him ask in faith, without doubting, because a person who doubts is like a wave of the sea that is driven and tossed by the wind. That person shouldn't suppose that he will receive anything from the Lord (James 1:5-6).

Here, you see how doubt hinders prayer. God wants you to trust Him, asking Him for those things you desire, believing He is capable of answering and that He will answer in the best way (whether His answer is "yes, no, or wait awhile").

Doubt is a moral issue because, like Adam's sin, it involves questioning God's Word. It creates a problem between you and God that must be resolved. The problem, therefore, must be resolved, not merely on the intellectual level—by acquiring more facts—but, as James makes clear, by repentance (see James 4:8-10).

Similarly, if you approach preaching doubting God's Word, do you think the Spirit of God will automatically teach and change you just because you were under the preaching of the Word? Your relationship toward God must be right for that. You must believe Him. You must come in a receptive frame of mind. You must be willing and anxious to learn all you can from God and desire to integrate it into your life. Any lesser approach to preaching is likely to be totally ineffective.[2]

This is, in effect, what Paul meant when he wrote that an elder must be "teachable" (1 Tim. 3:2).[3] What is true of the elder, as the example to the flock, should be true of all believers. Teachableness is a fundamental quality of learning. It involves more than a desire to hear new things (the Athenians had that: Acts 17:21). Curiosity, though a small element in teachableness, is not enough. There must be a burning desire to know God better, to please Him more often, to serve Him more adequately. That is at the bottom of biblical teachableness. Many people are anxious to know more—to satisfy natural curiosity, to gain the power that knowledge brings, etc. But learning is a moral-spiritual matter because it involves motive. What is your motive in listening to a sermon? That is the question to answer.

When your motive is right, your heart is humble, and your relationship is otherwise proper toward God, you will be ready to listen; but not before. It is important then not to arrive at church after some last-minute sweep out of the bed, through the kitchen, and into the car—like Dagwood

Bumstead late for work. It is important to spend some time beforehand preparing yourself to receive God's message. Indeed, if the problem between you and God is serious enough, you may find it necessary to spend the previous day setting it right. If that isn't possible, it may be necessary to see your pastor for counseling. But, whatever it takes, the important thing is to be prepared: you are going to church to hear God's message to you!

Expectations
Though much more could be written about your spiritual state, what has been said will have to do. Closely related to this topic is the matter of expectations. If you go to church with the attitude, *O well, I guess all we can expect this morning is another boring sermon,* then you are more than likely to find your expectations fulfilled. On the other hand, if you say to yourself, *This morning God has a message for me that should change my life,* then those expectations will certainly be fulfilled.

The excitement of a sermon comes not from novelty or sensationalism, but from the true vitality of the Word as it is faithfully preached in the power of the Spirit (1 Cor. 2:1-3). But wrong expectations can stifle truth. *Expect* something fresh, something important, something exciting—from *God!*

The Israelites who urged their friends to listen to Ezekiel, in expectation of hearing a preacher who was "like a lovely song, sung with a beautiful voice and played well on an instrument" (Ezek. 33:32, BERK), listened for the wrong purpose. They wanted to be entertained. They were neither interested in what Ezekiel had to say nor willing to obey the Word of God he preached. Their hearts were "set on their own selfish gain" (Ezek. 33:31, BERK).

Those concerned with the preacher, rather than God— even when they commend him for his ability to use words well—come to church for the wrong reasons. It was against such attitudes that Christ spoke so strongly at Nazareth. There He condemned the synagogue community for focusing on the fact that He was the home-town boy made good (Luke 4:22) rather than listening to the message He was delivering. By doing so, they missed the stupendous truth He proclaimed. If, then, it is wrong to focus expectations on the preacher, even when you expect his sermon to be exciting or entertaining, how much more so when your expectations are negative?

The whole point is this: when you go to hear a sermon, you must be concerned about one thing: what does God have to say to me? Focus on God. See preaching as a transaction not merely between yourself and the preacher, but between yourself and God. The preacher is a means to that end. Go expecting to hear a Word from God that, when obeyed, will change your life.[4] Lesser expectations will not do.

I have sat in the pew long enough to know it can be irritating when the sermon is halting or superficial, but if you are an alert listener who is anxious to receive a message from God, you will rarely go away disappointed. Even on those rare occasions when the sermon is a total disaster, which I shall consider in a later chapter, you can take action to realize your expectations.

Predisposition

Many items could be addressed under the heading of predisposition. But, here, I want to mention only one: *childlikeness* (not childishness). Jesus often spoke of this quality (see, for instance, Matt. 18:3). What element in a child was Jesus commending? Possibly there was more than one. But, surely, the one quality that is so sorely needed today in our super-sophisticated society is a fresh openness to new facts, combined with a willingness to believe. This combination produces a *sense of wonder*.

This sense of wonder must be maintained at all times. It's loss largely contributes to the boredom that is described in the words *old hat*. F.W. Boreham, whose sermons are widely known, spoke of the need for this childlike wonder when he wrote:

And yet, after all, I suppose it was largely my fault that the sermon of which I have spoken seemed to me to be so ineffective. There are tremendous astonishments in the Christian evangel which, however badly stated, should fire my sluggish soul with wonder, and fill it with amazement. The fact that I listened so blandly shows that I have become blasé. I am like the soldier in the trenches who no longer notices the bursting shells about him. I am like the auditor who occupies a seat at a conjuring entertainment, but has fallen asleep just as the thing is getting sensational.[5]

The blasé predisposition ("I've heard it all before") is dangerous not only for the soldier in the trenches, but also for the listener in the pew. It is always dangerous to take God for granted.

We live in a world of amazing discoveries. I am typing this manuscript on a word processor. It is an amazing piece of equipment! Yet, I have learned to take it for granted. Perhaps the problem is just that: because we take so many amazing things happening around us as a matter of course, we are predisposed to do so with the wonderful words of God. What can be done about this?

The answer is to recapture the childlike predisposition you once had. Studies show, that, on the whole, children are better listeners than adults.[6] Adults are persons who have learned not to listen. When you were a little child, each blade of grass, each bug crawling on it, each vein on a leaf was an entrancing discovery. Your eyes and ears were wide open to the world around. Few things escaped you. Lights at night entranced you, soft breezes playing on your hair in the evening captivated you. But now, engrossed in more important things, you have learned to block out much of your world. The capacity to do this is God-given, and not necessarily wrong. Some of the dreamy persons who accomplish so little in this world, have been *overcome* by this quality of wonder. That is not what I am talking about. But the other extreme to which most of us are acclimated, is every bit as bad: few things shock, amaze, cause us to stop and think—or meditate. That is bad, very bad. Read Mark 11:25; Luke 10:21.

Hurricane Hugo devastated the Virgin Islands, Puerto Rico, and the Carolina coast. The San Francisco/Oakland/ Santa Cruz earthquake rocked the nation. It takes events as catastrophic as these to make an impact on most of us today. Perhaps that is one reason in God's providence why such things happen! They wake us up and shake us out of our lethargy, shattering modern over-sophistication that we have allowed to make us blasé.

"I see that," you say. "In fact, I experience it in my own life. But how can I overcome it?"

I suggest two things: (1) learn how to do in-depth Bible study; (2) learn to appreciate all the wonders around you as part of the creation of Almighty God and the outworking of His providence.

Most Christians study their Bibles superficially. They think that they have it all together after hearing a few sermons, reading a few superficial books, and studying for a few weeks with a group of others who are pooling ignorance and writing superficial answers in the white spaces of booklets that actually teach you how *not* to study the Bible.

What you need is more in-depth study. This book is not the place to teach you how to do this. I would refer you to my book, *What to Do on Thursday* (Phillipsburg: Presbyterian and Reformed Publishing Co., 1982) for further help. Or you may ask your pastor to develop and teach a course for you and others who may be interested. My point here is that you will find it difficult to become blasé when you begin to see something of the multiplicity of matters in the Bible that you never recognized before. When you begin to grapple with the problems of understanding and interpretation that face all who *study* its pages. When you learn so much more of His will for you and measure your feeble attempts to conform against its magnificent portrait of the righteous life of Christ. In study of this sort, you will be stumbling over new truth, new insights, new life applications all the time. And you'll take this freshness of interest and ability with you when you go to hear the Word preached. In-depth Bible study, conducted wisely, will reawaken the childlike sense of awe and wonder.

My other suggestion is to open yourself to all the wonders of God's creation and providence surrounding you. The key here is to see the computer (or whatever) not solely as an invention of man—that leads to the blasé attitude. Rather, you must see that in His providence God has brought this invention into common use at this time, for His own purposes. Again, see Him as being active in society. Ask yourself: *How can a computer be used for the propagation of the Gospel? How may I use it in my limited sphere to honor Him and bless others?* Think of it as we now think of the printing press which, providentially, appeared just when the Reformers needed it to spread the truth.

Begin to experience the world as the handiwork of God, everyday life as His hand now at work. Learn how "the earth is His, and the fulness thereof" (Ps. 24:1). In other words, begin to see afresh that God is at work, sustaining and guiding the world and all that is in it. See Him even turning the wrath of man to His praise (Ps. 76:10). When you experience the world with the childlike sense attuned to God's presence, greatness, and all-pervasiveness in life, once again you will experience that childlike sense of wonder. Indeed, you will experience a greater fascination with life than you knew as a child, because in it all you will become fascinated with God. Cynicism will pass, the grinding toil of routine will be superceded, and life will take on a new sheen. Then you will go to preaching to find out more about this amazing God whose words and works you have been tracking throughout the week in substantive Bible study, with senses attuned to His presence. You will want to learn how better to please Him. You will have the proper disposition to get the most out of preaching. You will come away aglow.

Work at Getting the Message

It may be superfluous to say so, but the whole point of listening is to get the message. Yet, were you to ask a handful of members leaving church on any Sunday morning what God's message was, not all (perhaps only a few) could tell you. Not all the fault for that lies with the preacher. Frequently, people missed Jesus' message during His ministry on earth; often they misconstrued it. If this happened to the Master, surely His servants can expect no more.

Summary Sentences
Let me suggest, therefore, that during every message you should constantly seek to discover God's message in the verse or verses from which it was preached, going so far as to summarize it in one sentence (which you might even determine to write out). Unless you can do this, it is doubtful whether you got the message.

What would these sentences look like? They need be nothing pretentious. They could be jotted down in rough form at church and revised more carefully at home. They will give you something to meditate on during the week. Here are some simple samples:

God wants me to give cheerfully.

God urges me to trust Him in times of suffering.

God calls on me to repent of doubt.

In all of these, you will notice, I have used the words *God* and

me. That sets up the fact that the sermon is a personal transaction that places responsibility on us as the recipients of a
message from our Creator and Saviour.

When you can accurately write out crisp sentences like
these, after the sermon, you can be reasonably certain that
you got the message. And, taking upon yourself this obligation will force you to listen more carefully, keep you off side-
tracks, and help you formulate the message in a short, porta-
ble form that you can readily recall for use.

Aggressive Listening

You will notice, however, that in suggesting this, I am asking
you to *work!* That is a new concept to many Christians. They
think that sermons provide time to lean back and listen pas-
sively, letting the preacher do all the work. But good listening is not passive; it requires effort. Effective listening calls
for aggressive mental activity: "A discerning mind *gets* knowledge and the ear of the wise *seeks* information" (Prov. 18:15,
BERK [emphasis mine]).

The two operative verbs in that sentence have to do with
energetic mental activity motivated by intense desire. Listeners must not assume the slovenly mental posture of a TV
couch potato. Their mere presence will not cause them to
absorb truth by some process of spiritual osmosis. It might
help to know that the definition of osmosis is: The passage of
a liquid or a fluid through a semi-permeable membrane, the
direction of the flow being from the less dense to the *more
dense substance!*

There is a well-known story about Calvin Coolidge, a man
of few words, who returned from church one day and was
asked by his sick wife, "What was the sermon about?"

Calvin answered, "Sin."

His wife persisted: "What did the minister say?"

"He was against it," Calvin replied.

In words nearly that concise, you should be able to briskly
summarize any message.

Too often those who complain that they are "not being

fed" really mean that they are not being *spoon-fed.* They expect the preacher to do all the work for them. They expect him to apply the passage *specifically* to exact situations, answering all possible questions and suggesting various applications and implementations that pertain precisely to them. In other words, they expect him to do all the work. Selfishly, they forget that there are other people in the congregation and that the preacher cannot think solely of their particular circumstances. I have had women complain because too many of my illustrations pertain to men, and others complain because too many illustrations pertain to women. The first group think I care only about men; the second believe I am sexist and only want to take it out on women. (I often hear this complaint even when my illustrations put women in a highly favorable light!) You can't win for losing with people like these. To expect *them* to apply general principles to the particulars of their lives, however, is too much. That's work! So, they declare, "We are not being fed."

And, people of this sort are often the first to complain when the preacher uses an example which, if they miss (or misconstrue) its point, can be used wrongly. Yet Christ was not afraid to tell a parable about an unjust judge, which some might infer depicts God as unjust (Luke 18:2ff). He didn't take the edge off the story by saying, "Now, you understand, of course, that I used an unjust judge in this story, not to represent God as such, but merely to compose a story in which I could make the point that people should pray continually."

No. He expected His listeners to use the brains with which God equipped them to figure that out for themselves.

Jesus did this sort of thing all the time. He spoke, for instance, of "hating" father, mother, brother, sister, and cutting off hands and feet. He told a parable in which He likened Himself to a hard master who picked up what he didn't put down and reaped what he didn't sow—*all* without the slightest explanation or qualification. He would not blur these vivid, powerful, memorable images that way. To do so would be like explaining the punch line of a joke. He simply left these parables, and dozens of other such sayings like them, just as He spoke them—running the risk of being misunderstood by lazy people who didn't want to think and being misinterpreted by picky people who wanted to excuse their failure to comply with God's words. Preaching like Christ's calls on people to bring their brains to church—and to *use* them.

Many congregations today have a hard time handling preaching like this. They don't want to take the trouble to understand hyperbole (a favorite device Christ used in preaching), figures of speech, or other vivid language. Some are so far gone that they won't even be spoon-fed; they require an IV!

The very language of this favorite word *fed* suggests passivity. Adults don't need to be fed; lead them to the green grass and they will feed themselves. That is the sense in which the preacher is to *feed* the flock. But the way people often use the word indicates they are immature and want someone else to do all their thinking for them. Mature Christians have learned to sit down at a sermon, as at a dinner table, help themselves to the shrimp, peel it, and feed themselves. In Hebrews 5, the writer calls lazy listeners babies that "need someone to teach [them] the basic elements of God's revelation once again" (v. 12).

This is because they are "inexperienced with the righteous Word" (v. 13), and their faculties have not been "trained to distinguish good from evil" (v. 14).

Such people, he says, are "dull in *hearing*" (v. 11). The word *dull* means "sluggish," and sometimes, in medical treatises of the day, the word means "comatose." It is not only preachers who are dull! Could it be, that when you find preaching dull, it is because of your own dullness—at least, in part?

When Jesus said, "Be careful how you hear" (Luke 8:18), among other things, He was urging us to diligently attend to God's message. Indeed, He insisted: "Hear and understand" (Matt. 15:10). But understanding requires thinking, and thinking means work. This process is summed up in the English word *attend*, the etymology of which says it all. The word comes from two Latin terms *ad* ("to"), and *tendo* ("stretch" or "bend"). To attend, therefore, is "to stretch" (or "bend") the mind to what another is saying. It is to reach out with all your mental and spiritual powers to grasp the meaning of the message. The word describes strong, mental effort expended to understand.

The words *viewer* or *spectator* describe the opposite. Yet, possibly because they have developed TV habits, many today drift into church with their minds turned off, slouch in the pew, and expect the preacher to do the rest. Examine yourself, brother or sister: have you been guilty of becoming a Sunday morning version of the couch potato? When should you most fully *attend* to what another has to say? Isn't it when he is presenting a message from God?

Summarizing a Poorly Organized Sermon

Suppose you recognize the advantage of summarizing God's basic message in a crisp sentence, but the sermon seems to contain more than one—it has little unity. Some preachers put too many thoughts into one sermon and end up saying very little about any one topic. This is because either their material is thin, or they have never learned that you can say more about less. Whatever the reason, it is true that you may often listen to what purports to be a message, but in reality turns out to be several messages. What do you do then?

Of course you may do many things. But, here is one suggestion: jot down a summary sentence for *each* of the two or three messages contained in the sermon. Then, choose *one* on which to concentrate your thinking, praying, and daily living for the coming week. Although this sort of preaching is usually poor, if you are willing to do some work, you can turn it to your advantage. You can choose the one message that is especially appropriate to you at the moment. Then, you can buy (borrow from the church library, etc.) some commentaries, Bible dictionaries, and other materials that enlarge on the message that the preacher did not have time to develop fully enough because he spent his time trying to do too many things.

In addition, you might make an appointment with the preacher to discuss more specifically the one message you chose. If you have done your homework in preparation, you might take with you a list of questions[1] that his message (and your later study and reflection) trigger, but that his message did not address. In this way, you will get the benefit you would have received if the preacher had preached only one message in greater depth and, to boot, you will be able to ask specific questions pertaining directly to your own situation. It is also possible that if you do this often enough (but be sure not to burden the pastor), or if enough members of the congregation do this, you may soon find your preacher learning to cover fewer points in greater depth.

But notice once again, all this requires work. The sort of listening that I am suggesting is like the listening of the Bereans, who, according to Acts 17:11 examined the Scriptures daily in response to what they heard. They were not viewers or spectators, listeners in the passive sense—they were active participants in Paul's preaching. They assumed they had a part to play and a responsibility to participate, and they did—*daily*. They worked at listening. No wonder so many believed!

Looking for Clues

"But how do I get at this message? I've never been very good at that sort of thing in school."

Let me suggest one thing you may find helpful: listen for clues. In an interesting experiment on listening, a group was asked to listen to the distorted tape recording of a talk. At first, the listeners couldn't make heads or tails out of it. But, given the clue, "It's about a tailor discussing a suit," they were then able to understand a good bit of it, in spite of the distortion.[2]

Sometimes, even before the preaching of the sermon you

can pick up most of the clues you need to zero in on the main message. Look at the church bulletin. Does the title give you a clue? What about the passage of Scripture that was read? And the hymns sung? Many pastors are quite careful to coordinate the various parts of the service with the message for the day. Often, in singing a hymn, they may even point out one verse that they want you to think about. All these elements can be rich sources of clues.

Indeed, sometimes you can even anticipate the message before you go to church. If your pastor is preaching through a book of the Bible, why not read the next chapter during the week? And, if his message titles are published in the newspaper, check them out ahead of time (these often appear on Fridays or Saturdays). You might also do some preliminary thinking about the passage, jotting down questions that come to mind. Carried with you on Sunday, these will help orient you to the thrust of the message. But, again, all this means you are going to have to do some work!

Types of Messages
It can be helpful to understand that a preacher's messages fall into one of three (nonexclusive) categories. They will be largely informative, persuasive (urging you to believe or disbelieve something) or motivational (urging you to do something). Good persuasive messages include information along with argumentation from the Scriptures. And good motivational messages add emotional appeal. All true messages are designed to change you in some way. Ask yourself, *How does God want me to be different after listening to this message?* Your answer may be *He wants me to know* _____ *(something I did not know before)*. If so, the message was informative. You may also answer, *He wants me to believe* _____ *(a certain truth)*. If so, the message was persuasive. Finally, you may respond *He wants me to do* _____ *(take a certain action)*. If so, the message was motivational.[3] A message on 1 Thessalonians 4:13 would be largely informative, one on John 20:31 (and the book as a

whole) would be persuasive (to convince), and a message on Jude 3 would be motivational.

"But," you ask, "how can I do all these things while I am trying to listen to the preacher? Won't I distract myself if I attempt to think about the main message and sum it up as an informative, persuasive, or motivational message in one crisp sentence?"

No, after you get the hang of it, you shouldn't. The speed at which we think is at least 4–5 times greater than the speed at which we speak. That is one reason why your thoughts tend to drift: you have time to spare. And you *will* do something with that extra time—daydream, think about a problem at work, etc. You would do better to spend extra time evaluating what the preacher is saying, looking for and formulating the main message, and thinking about how your life ought to be different for having heard the sermon.

"OK," you may say. "All this is helpful when the message is pertinent. But how about all those messages that don't have anything to do with me, hold no particular interest for me, or are just a repetition of something I've heard again and again?"

Everything in the Bible is pertinent to you *in some way*. Yes, even if you are a single person, sermons on marriage can be pertinent. They can help prepare you for the future, or, if there is no likelihood of marriage ever occurring, they can orient you to some of the difficulties that married people must overcome (so that you can become more tolerant of them when you see them struggling to do so). Part of the challenge of listening to something that does not *immediately* seem pertinent to you is to work at making it so. Even the seemingly most remote messages can become vital to you.

Sure, there are messages in which you are not interested.[4] But nothing in God's Word may be overlooked. It is all there for a purpose, and it all can become interesting to you. Again, it is *your* task to make it so. You must take an interest in it. You know, as well as I do, that people listen to what they are interested in. Just let someone mention your name in a group on the other side of the room, and a conversation to which you were not listening immediately becomes interesting. You prick up your ears to find out what they are saying about you.

One way to become interested is to ask yourself why you are not interested. Could it be that you avoid certain areas of biblical truth because of some sin in your life that you are unwilling to give up? Are you otherwise biased against the truth? Do you misunderstand it? Taking an interest in your lack of interest can create great interest!

You're not particularly interested in the Amalekites? Well, then, *take* an interest in the biblical account of God's people and the Amalekites. Don't rest until you discover how the story of the Amalekites can be of benefit to you this coming week. Work at the passage until it becomes vital to you. If the immediate subject itself is not of interest, as preached, don't give up until you have made it so.

And, then, what of repetitive material—the message that you have heard over and over again? Even if there is not a single new word spoken (a rarity), concentrate on how *you* can make the old, old story new to yourself, or to others. Think of at least three new applications, new insights, or new angles that you can mention to others after the service ("You know, Jane, during the message this morning something the pastor said reminded me that if we were only to do so-and-so in our women's group....") Perhaps you can be a great blessing to others in this way, helping them to expand their horizons, and pointing them to ways of utilizing old truths in new ways.

What I have been saying is that you must learn to be much more creative and flexible in your listening. But, as I have repeated throughout the chapter, that means you must *work*. If you don't, you will not get the message. The natural processes of selectivity, drift, and entropy will win out.

CHAPTER SEVEN

Understanding the Message

The point of the Parable of the Sower (Matt. 13:3ff) is to encourage you to *hear with understanding.* As His text for this discourse, Jesus quotes Isaiah 6:9-10: "This people's heart has become dull . . . hard of hearing" (Matt. 13:15). Isaiah explains that while people hear with their ears, many do not "understand with their heart" (v. 15). They hear, but don't hear—i.e., they hear words but they don't understand them (v. 17).

King James II commanded an act of parliament to be read in all the churches. Preachers who disagreed didn't want to read it, and members of their churches didn't want to hear it. So one pastor told his people, "Though I am compelled to read this, you are not compelled to hear it." His congregation walked out. He then read the act to empty pews. Many today listen as if they were not compelled to do so; preachers preach as if to empty pews. Jesus' parable requires something more.

In the interpretation of the parable, Jesus speaks of the failure of some to understand the message (v. 19) but also of those who "bear fruit" because they do understand (v. 23). What He is teaching, among other things is that there are various hindrances to understanding. When the seed is sown, it falls on three sorts of nonreceptive hearts:

● Hard, stony hearts, on which the seed is wasted. Such hearers don't even listen.

● Superficial hearts, not deep enough for a plant to grow in. Such hearers don't grasp the meaning of the truth they hear.

● Worldly hearts, in which weeds of worry and avarice

choke out all growth. Such hearts have no room for the message.

Thus hostility, emotionalism, and idolatry all mitigate the productive sowing of God's truth. Such things make one sermon-proof.

Against these three kinds of soil, Jesus places the "good" soil. This soil represents those who "hear the Word" and also "hold on to it" (Luke 8:15). They are also those who hear and understand (Matt. 13:23).

In this chapter we shall consider the three hindrances to understanding, and what it takes to "understand" or "hold on to" truth. While the three hindrances to understanding characterize unbelievers, remnants of each continue to plague believers as well. Surely, if you look within your heart, you will agree.

Resistance
This problem is so serious in the unregenerate person that Paul tells us "The natural person doesn't welcome the things of God's Spirit" (1 Cor. 2:14). We looked at this problem in detail in Chapter 1. While no true Christian can totally reject God's message, as unbelievers reject the Gospel, Christians do still struggle with residual resistance to biblical teaching that runs contrary to the self-centered ways, developed while still in unbelief.[1] Wide acceptance and propagation of humanistic ideas of self-worth, self-esteem, and self-image in the evangelical church have served to aggravate the problem.

Mark knows that his involvement in pornography is wrong, that by it he is committing adultery of the heart. Yet, he persists, rejecting clear preaching against sexual sin. Indeed, he goes about slandering the pastor before other members of the congregation with such innuendos as "the preacher preaches too much about sex, don't you think? I wonder if he has a problem in this area?"

Mark is holding out, unwilling to deal with sin in his life. He resists, therefore, the plain preaching of the Word whenever the preacher approaches his sin. Others may not slander the preacher, but they may rationalize and make excuses. Florence thinks, "Sure, I ought to submit to my husband. And, I would . . . if he would only take the headship in our home." Such resistance is no less serious.

Christian, do you listen to preaching with a heart wide open to truth, a heart unprotected from thrusts of the Spirit's sword? Or is your heart hard, resistant to certain teaching? Have you so rationalized your sin that your conscience rarely, if ever, accuses you of certain sins anymore? Then it is time to repent, saying with David, "Search me, O God, and know my heart!" (Ps. 139:23) It is time to crack open those compartments of the heart that you have so successfully barred. Instead, bare them to the preaching of the Word. Listen with a willingness to hear, understand, apply, and obey. Until you do, preaching will be virtually valueless to you. A resistant heart may be the very problem that stands in the way of joyful hearing of the Word.

Superficiality
Quickly accepted, quickly rejected (or, as we say: "in one ear and out the other") seems to be the problem of the person represented by the second soil. It is the problem of superficiality, lack of depth. *Sure the Gospel sounds good; I'll add it, along with everything else, to my life.* So thinks the unregenerate person. And, much modern preaching, which ignores the need for repentance, only encourages this kind of thinking.

Such people don't resist the truth because they don't know enough about it to do so. If they really understood the Word, they would reject it out of hand because they would realize that the Gospel of Jesus Christ leads to a thorough change of life (Eph. 4:17). Radical change is the very last thing a superficial person wants. He will settle for Christianity only as an add-on. The only difficulty is that the One who said "Choose this day whom you will serve" and who scathingly asked "Why are you limping between two opinions?" (like a lame man who leans first this way and then that as he walks) won't have it that way (1 Kings 18:21).

But, as the history of Israel makes abundantly clear, some of that spirit can linger in believers hindering even God's people. Genuine Christians, who fail to think through the implications of sound preaching, often find that they start out joyfully on an endeavor, only to quit when they encounter the first bump in the road. On the one hand, they may fail to understand because they do not penetrate to the depths of what is preached, settling for a superficial understanding (misunderstanding) of the message or, on the other hand, giving too quick an assent to truth without bothering to understand the life commitment that it implies. As a result, they either take wrong turns or, having headed in the right direction, give up when the going gets rough. In either case, superficial understanding (of what the truth is, or what it demands of them) leads to faulty responses to preaching.

Understanding isn't being able to repeat the words of the catechism or memorizing verses for the next Bible quiz. When about to go overseas, we taught our children some minimal words in several languages (*dove la gabenetta*, etc.). Years later a child from a Christian home was visiting us. One of our children asked, "Parlez vous francais?" The friend replied, "I haven't learned that catechism question yet!"

Fred listens to preaching the way I collect coins and stamps: casually. I take whatever comes. If a letter from a foreign country arrives, I cut off the stamp, throw it into an envelope and promptly forget about it. I do the same with coins and bills from overseas: whatever remains in my pocket after an overseas trip goes into a box. Occasionally, I discover unusual American coins. Again, off they go into a box. Why? Because I have only a superficial interest in them. *Perhaps someday*, I tell myself, *if I ever get the time, I'll become a serious stamp collector — or collector of coins. Or, possibly, one of my grandchildren will take up the hobby, and I'll have something to help get him started.* Fred does the same with God's truth.

God doesn't want your superficial, casual concern. He wants you to become the kind of dedicated, knowledgeable collector of truth who understands it for use in life and ministry. Serious stamp and coin collecting is hard work! You have to give thought, time and effort to the project. Listening to sermons properly is solid work; it takes dedication, searching for missing elements in the fabric of truth. The superficial hearer knows little of this.

Christian, can you say that you devote even so much time to understanding truth and its implications for life as you do to a hobby? If you are willing to spend more time learning how to play golf, there is something radically wrong with your priorities. But, it may be, you don't even spend time with hobbies or sports. You are just lazy. Face it. God says to wake up (Rom. 13:11; Heb. 12:12-13) and get to work! He wants no Christians to be lazy about their faith. While He requires no one to be an enthusiastic stamp collector, or fisherman, He does require all Christians to enthusiastically work at their faith. Enthusiasm isn't enough, however. That soon wears thin. The superficial hearer often gets all excited about what he hears—until he discovers that he must commit himself, discipline himself in pursuit of righteousness, and expend great amounts of time and energy.

Worldliness
It is interesting that Jesus speaks of worldliness in this context not so much in terms of activities, but in terms of one's life orientation (as He does also in Matt. 6:19ff.). His emphasis is on where we focus our concerns: on the things the Gentiles seek (food, clothing, and what money can buy) or on the kingdom of God. Again, it is a matter of priorities—what one seeks *first* (Matt. 6:33). When things come first, like weeds, they choke the Word that is sown. They crowd out biblical teaching so that there is little room for it to grow and bear fruit.

Unlike the superficial hearer, these hearers are not lazy. They are zealously seeking—the wrong things. They are busily concerned about all sorts of things. The search for security in "things" is what creates insecurity. Security cannot be found in this world. When money, things, popularity, and power take first place, worries and cares, like weeds, grow thick.

Believers are not immune to the problem. They too struggle with noxious worldly growth that hinders the fruitful growth of the Word.

Jonathan's house is on the market. He must sell in the next three months or he will lose a sum of money he put down on a new place. Day and night this matter preys on his mind. It keeps him from sleeping properly; he spends time worrying about it that could be productively put to work in the Lord's vineyard. And even when he attends church, he can think of little that the preacher says because he is worrying about the sale of the house. Even his prayers are filled with this one matter, which seems to crowd out everything else. Jonathan has work to do in his heart—he needs to spread weedkiller generously.

The Understanding Heart

The "right sort of ground" is ground that receives the seed *with understanding* (Matt. 13:23). It is ground that Jesus describes as a "worthy and good heart." It is a heart that "holds on" to the seed and "perseveres" until it produces fruit (Luke 8:15). When truth sinks into the right sort of heart, one filled with good will toward God, anxious and ready to receive His Word and obey it, understanding springs forth. That is the heart of one who not only accepts truth but also *continues* to work with it until that truth has been integrated into life and ministry. The good (literally, "fine") listener takes the time to thoroughly digest and understand what God requires of him, counts the cost before putting it into practice, and perseveres in rehabituating his life until it conforms to God's truth. He gives God's Word priority over all other interests (even legitimate ones). He seeks not only God's kingdom, but also His righteousness. He pursues righteousness, not for personal benefit, but out of gratitude to God, "for His name's sake."

Because he wants very much to be like Christ, the person with a "fine heart" considers sowing (the preaching of the Word) an important factor in his life. He is faithful in his attendance at church and works at understanding what he hears. He believes (rightly) that receiving God's Word and acting on it promotes spiritual growth. Though he recognizes the difficulties in bringing about change, like a faithful farmer, he patiently commits himself to the hard work of cultivating spiritual fruit. He perseveres because he is anxious to produce a large crop—to the glory of God.

Like Daniel, the good listener *sets his heart* to understand God's truth (Dan. 10:12). There is, in those words, as there is in Luke 8:15, a determination to change and a commitment to it. That kind of person, like Ezra, has "set his heart to study the law of the Lord, to practice it, and to teach its statutes and ordinances" (Ezra 7:10).

No wonder Ezra became a ready (skillful) scribe (Ezra 7:6)!

God expects such commitment of *you*. Until you go to hear the preaching of the Word in that spirit, it will profit you very little. With Ezra-like determination you must never rest until you discover ways and means to understand and implement what you hear. Poor or inadequate preaching will not stop you. Nothing a preacher says that is out of kilter with the way you see things will turn you off. You will drain him dry, attempting to learn all you can from him. You will persist until you get to the bottom of misunderstandings and clear up puzzles. And, as you zealously do so, more and more you will realize the promise that "the Lord will give you understanding" (2 Tim. 2:7).

Of what does understanding consist? At least the following three elements:

- Hearing truth precisely;
- Processing truth properly;
- Storing truth for later use.

Luther said, "Understanding is . . . a careful retention of what has been received."[2]

In one way or another, each of these elements will be

considered in the remainder of the book, along with other matters, so I shall say nothing more of them here. Indeed, it is now time to fulfill a promise I made earlier when I said that I would tell you how to get something even from mediocre or downright poor preaching. That is the subject of the next chapter.

CHAPTER EIGHT

How to Handle Poor Preaching

Martin Luther wrote:

> Since the preachers have the office, the name and the honor of being God's co-workers, no one should think that he is so learned or so holy that he may despise or miss the most insignificant sermon. This is especially true because he does not know at what time the hour will come in which God will do His work in him through the preachers.[1]

The important problem I shall consider in this chapter is not what makes preaching poor, but how you respond when it is—how you respond to what Luther calls the "most insignificant sermon." Do you assume responsibility for getting something out of such a sermon, or do you blame a failure to do so wholly on the preacher? Do you turn away in disgust, saying, "Well, *that* was a waste of time," or do you turn a liability into an asset? Luther seems to think it possible.

"But I don't see how," you might reply. "After all, how can you get more out of a sermon than is there? And, I'm not only concerned about 'insignificant' sermons, but also outright poor ones—and, even heretical ones. What about those?"

In this chapter I shall take up all those problems.

Seeming Heresy
Bill and Mary were converted through the outreach of an evangelical church. They joined the church and spent three delightful years growing under the ministry of the Rev. John

Smith, their faithful pastor. Now, however, things have changed. Pastor Smith has retired and his position has been taken by Pastor Jones. At first, all seemed well. The transition was smooth. Pastor Jones is a likeable person and seems to be well received. But, lately, from the pulpit Bill and Mary have been hearing teaching, that, at best, they must call "suspect." It seems that certain statements made by the new minister imply that the Scriptures contain errors and cannot be relied on. In addition, they seem to detect a false gospel of salvation by works. Under such circumstances, what must they do?

First, they must make sure of their facts. How? Well, *not* by going around among other members of the congregation asking if they agree. That could be quite divisive if they are wrong. No. Instead, they should make an appointment with Pastor Jones himself and humbly voice their concerns. By "humbly," I mean showing respect for the office he holds and with recognition that they may be mistaken. They should approach him tentatively, not going so far as to accuse him of heresy. Perhaps they could say something like:

> Pastor, we may have misunderstood, but here is what we think you have been saying. Please tell us if we are wrong; we are deeply concerned about this. We have come to you first; we haven't made our concerns known to anyone else in the congregation.

If Pastor Jones is the right sort of man, he will commend them for their honesty and prudence and will listen carefully to them. Perhaps Jones' response will be satisfactory; there may truly have been misunderstandings (possibly he was talking about variant manuscript readings and stressing the need for fruit as evidence of repentance). Because of their visit, the pastor will probably make an effort to be clearer in his preaching. That alone will be to the benefit of the entire congregation. Perhaps, out of the interview, Bill and Mary will grow even more, learning about matters of which they had been somewhat ignorant before. All in all, such an encounter can be most salutary.

Of course, if they kept these concerns to themselves and simply left for another church, none of these good things would happen. And, if they went about the congregation, spreading their concerns, they might spread seeds of doubt that nothing will remedy.

Heresy

On the other hand, let us suppose that Jones' reply only confirms their suspicion. He tells them that they are trusting in the Bible as "a paper pope," and that the very idea that human beings have no merit to present to God in order to be saved is ludicrous. He might say:

> Human beings are God's masterpiece. They are godlike beings. The only problem is that they have not yet evolved to the place where they have thrown off all of their animal tendencies. That's what we mean by "sin."

A conversation like that means that Bill and Mary were right. Under such circumstances what should they do? Leave? No.

They have a further obligation. They must speak to the elders (or other board members, depending on the kind of church it may be) about the problem. They have a responsibility to the congregation and to the Lord that they cannot discharge by leaving the church. They should explain to the elders what they have heard, both in preaching and in conversation with the pastor. Because there are two of them, they are properly able to bring a charge against the pastor (1 Tim. 5:19). If the board deals with the matter and dismisses the pastor, again, all is well and—because they were careful hearers of the Word in preaching—Bill and Mary will have served their Lord and the congregation well.

But, let us now suppose that the board refuses to do anything about the matter. They say that they like Pastor Jones, that they think he may be right, and that Pastor Smith was old-fashioned. What should Bill and Mary do next?

Well, depending on the situation, they must do one of two things:

1. If the church belongs to a denomination it may be possible to appeal to a high body (a presbytery, convention, etc.). This may take time, and it will require patience on their part. But they are obligated to take every action possible to try to restore the ministry of this church. They should obtain a copy of the denominational form of government and follow the directions for appeal set forth *to the letter*. It is possible that, otherwise, their appeal may be disregarded on technical grounds.

2. If the church is independent, they must attempt to rally as many of the members of the congregation as possible to bring about a change in the situation — including not only a dismissal of the pastor, but also the dismissal of those official board members who countenanced error. That sort of thing can never be pleasant. They will be villified all along the way by some, but if they persist in a proper, humble, helpful manner, not returning evil for evil, but overcoming evil with good (Rom. 12:21), keeping Christ's honor and His church's welfare always uppermost in their minds, they will proceed rightly.

Now, in the event that none of these measures succeed, they must finally leave the church (if they have not already been put out). They must thereafter unite with a church in which the Gospel is preached and the Lord's Word is held inerrant. And, if the church has persisted in maintaining a false gospel, they must take as many others from the congregation as they can with them. If there is no other Bible-believing congregation in town, they may even find it necessary to start one themselves, perhaps appealing to a denomination that is faithful to the Scriptures to assist them.

Regardless of the final outcome, Mary and Bill will discover that, *if they have proceeded biblically* throughout the process, they will have grown immensely. But they must avoid all bitterness, and other non-Christian attitudes in everything they do and say. They must be sure that their motives are right—that they have not enjoyed the limelight into which this controversy has thrown them, etc. It would be well, if possible, for them to be counseled by mature Christians during the latter part of this affair, once it has become a public matter. It is so easy—especially for young Christians—to go wrong when going right!

Thin Soup
But, now, let's consider a wholly different situation. Pastor Jones' preaching is neither suspect nor heretical—just poor! Indeed, he talks about the wonderful truths of the Word as if they were the most dull and matter-of-fact issues. Pastor Smith was easy to listen to, helpful, and relevant. Bill and Mary always went away challenged and edified. Jones, on the other hand, is not only boring, but abstract and difficult to follow. He talks like a poorly written book rather than a human being, and he says virtually nothing worth carrying away for reflection. His preaching can best be described as thin soup served cold. W.R. Maltby described one preacher this way: "He spoke of great things and made them small, of holy things and made them common, of God and made Him of no account.[2] In such a case what should Bill and Mary do?

Checking through the chapters you have already read, you will discover not only important matters of attitude that they must remember, but several suggestions for making the most of poor preaching. In what follows I want to make other suggestions for handling preaching that is dull, disorganized, abstract, repetitious, shallow, full of truisms, clichés, etc. To some extent, these suggestions may be used in any number of situations hardly as bad as the one described in the previous paragraph. However, they must be used with care, always cheerfully expecting something better from the pulpit than the usual fare. After all, if you have been praying for Jones, you should look for answers. So, do not substitute what I am about to suggest for careful listening. These are last-resort suggestions—to be followed *only when all else has failed.* Let's assume you are Bill or Mary.

First, you should pray for Pastor Jones. The effectual, fervent prayer of a righteous person is powerful. It can even change preaching! God once asked Moses, "Who made man's mouth?" God can do something about Jones' preaching. Perhaps the pastor will become convicted about his ineptness and seriously work at improvement. He may buy books that will help, take courses, or attend seminars on preaching.

It is also possible that, if Jones really doesn't belong in the ministry, he will become aware of it and be relieved of a burden he should not try to bear.

It is also possible to become friendly enough with Jones to the point where you can talk directly to him about the problem. Perhaps you can provide the finances he needs to take courses in preaching, buy books, or whatever. Besides praying for him, ask yourself, "How can I help Jones to help us all?" More than one pastor has come to our doctoral program in preaching because his congregation sent him. As a result, many were able to find the help they needed. In everything, be as encouraging as possible. If your pastor has the gifts undeveloped, he will need encouragement, not the opposite.

Stopgap Measures
But, suppose you are praying, offering help, etc. and Jones is not getting better rapidly. What can you do in the meantime? Here are a few suggestions.

1. Look for main points in the message, or—if there are none to speak of—points suggested by the message. Jot down questions, observations, illustrations, and key passages that might relate to these main points. Then, when you get home, study them more carefully using a concordance, Bible dictionaries, and commentaries. Even good preachers encourage such study. In a sermon, Augustine (one of the three great preachers of the post-Apostolic Age) once said, "I have flung out a few hints...take them and work out the rest for yourselves."[3] You will find that there is more to the morning message than you thought—suggestively, at least, and you will be on your way to becoming a serious Bible student. It may be that in His providence God sent Pastor Jones to make Bible students out of this congregation.

2. *Ask yourself, "Now, how would I approach that passage?"* In doing so, you may get leads on your personal study of which you never dreamed. You will find that you are working all the harder because the pastor isn't (or doesn't know how to) work that hard to understand the Scriptures or communicate his understanding to others.

3. *Take more notes than you would otherwise.* Many people take too many notes and thereby distract themselves. They should be exhorted to write down only new or questionable data. But there is little from which to be distracted with Pastor Jones; therefore, take notes on all that comes into your mind. Make the time profitable. Meditate, and take notes on that. Question, and note your questions, etc.

4. *Think of your life in relationship to the sermon (or your reconstruction of it).* Personalize all abstractions. Ask, "How does God want me to be different for having been here today?" Try to discover why the Holy Spirit put the passage in the Bible. Ask, "What is the Holy Spirit trying to do?" Reflect on this specifically in relationship to your own life and determine at least three ways in which you can implement the Holy Spirit's purpose during the coming week.

5. *On an especially bad day, forget about the sermon and focus on a hymn, the Scripture reading, or something in the prayer that rings a bell.* Then, in relation to this, or several of these, do some of the things suggested in points 1–4.

6. *When working through a problem of heresy or error in a sermon (perhaps while awaiting the board or the denomination's decision about Jones), what do you do? Simple. You learn from the sermon by contrast.* When error is preached, ask, "What

does the Bible really say?" Pursue that line until you are sure of the biblical truth. You will be especially sharpened if you read solid books that will help keep you straight. And you will need to know what you are talking about when you face the board or the denominational leaders. The process will prepare you.

7. *Remember what it must have been like for Jesus to sit under the atrocious preaching of the synagogue for thirty years!*

What all this amounts to is taking seriously the doctrine of the priesthood of all believers, for which the reformers fought. They asserted not only the right but also the responsibility of the individual believer to come directly to God in prayer and to study the Bible on his own. An authoritative church tried to stop them—and failed! God's Word and God's Spirit are of greater authority. Yet, having said that, it is also important to observe that Jesus gave His church pastors and teachers to aid believers in fulfilling their responsibility (Eph. 4:11-12). Because all believers have direct access to God and the Bible is no reason for us to despise or neglect the ministry of the Word that our Lord established for our benefit. And Spurgeon could not have been too far from the truth when he said, "I have listened to many sermons from preachers called poor, in all corners of the country, and I never heard one that did not teach me something, if I was in the spirit to profit from it."[4] But, all of this leads to the matter of hearing like a Berean, which is the subject of the next chapter.

CHAPTER NINE
Berean Listening

The priesthood of all believers—mentioned at the conclusion of the last chapter—means not only that Christians have the privilege of direct access to God in prayer and in the interpretation of the Scriptures, but it also implies an accompanying individual responsibility. I have mentioned a number of aspects of that responsibility already, but in this chapter I shall develop just one: the responsibility of every Christian to distinguish truth from error, a responsibility that extends to listening to preaching.

When John wrote, "Now you have an Anointing from the Holy One and you know all truth" (1 John 2:20), he was referring to the Holy Spirit whom Jesus sent to dwell within each Christian. Because He is the Spirit of truth (John 16:13), the ultimate Author of Scripture, and the One who illumines those who rightly study it, believers *potentially* possess "all truth." That is an amazing, heartening fact. Certainly none of us ever realizes that potential in this life, yet John tells us that it exists.

In another book, he writes: "the Anointing that you received from Him remains in you and you don't need anybody to teach you. Rather . . . His Anointing teaches you about everything" (1 John 2:27). Now from this we understand that the Spirit is the final source of truth, that He teaches you, and that when it comes down to the wire, even God-given teachers (though helpful, and important) are not absolutely necessary. A Christian on a desert island with only his Bible could learn to worship and serve God.

Although teachers are important, God holds you responsible to determine whether what they say is accurate (see

1 John 4:1 and Deuteronomy 13:1-5. Note, in each case, it is the teaching supporting their claims that you must examine).

"But how can individual Christians decide? By what standard may one judge the truth of what is preached?"

We can decide the same way the Bereans did, using the same standard they used:

> Now those Jews were more noble than those in Thessalonica, and they received the Word with great eagerness, examining the Scriptures daily to see if these things were so. As a result, many of them believed (Acts 17:11-12).

Notice the combination of eagerness and critical judgment among the Bereans. Personal biases that might intrude — such as those expressed at Thessalonica — were absent. The Bereans had a bias toward truth; toward biblical preaching. But they also had a bias against anything else.

When the Bereans heard the biblical message, they were excited over it. They assumed the responsibility God laid on them in Deuteronomy 13 and determined to see if what they heard was true. And, they knew where to turn to do so — the Bible. Their knowledge seems to have been exceeded only by their eagerness to learn. In Berean-like spirit, Augustine once urged his congregation to attend preaching "with burning thirst and fervent hearts."[1] This eagerness led the Bereans to devote all their spare time to the matter: they "examined the Scriptures daily." And, as a result, many believed.

A Berean Mentality

Two attitudes flourish among Bible searchers. Some may search the Scriptures, eager to discover the preacher was wrong. That is *not* the Berean spirit. Rather, they diligently searched the Scriptures because they were eager to discover truth. While the search for truth is sure to uncover error at times and it is important to know how to distinguish the one from the other[2], the way you approach the problem is all-important.

Some have developed a mentality that says, "I can't wait to find something wrong!" And, because we are all sinners, including every preacher, usually some error can be found in even the best preaching. The Berean-like searcher says, "I can't wait to find something new from God!"

Critical Thinking

While those with the latter mentality are eager, they are not naive. The Bereans eagerly received God's truth but only after systematic, daily efforts to ascertain that what the preacher said was biblical.

The standard, against which the Berean Jews measured truth, was the Scriptures. They did not say, "The preacher seems sincere," or, "He is more intelligent than I." They didn't say, "These would be nice teachings to adopt; they make me feel good." And they didn't say, "I know this preacher is right because of the experiences I have had since I believed." No. They did not base their acceptance of new teaching on the kind of man they supposed the preacher to be (recent events involving television preachers have vividly shown how perilous that can be), on feelings (they can change with the weather) or on experience (any Wednesday, you can hear about "glorious experiences" in a Christian Science testimony meeting). Laying aside these false, subjective standards—which are all too frequently adopted by uncritical Christians—the Bereans tested everything by the objectively given Bible. And that is just what God, who commends these Bereans, expects you to do.

Childlikeness, mentioned in an earlier chapter, must not be pushed to the point of absurdity and irresponsibility. One aspect of childlikeness is willingness to believe. If you tell a child that a little green man lives in the radio and makes it work, he will believe you. Surely, that is not what Jesus meant when He told us to become like little children. The passage in Acts 17 makes it clear that it is not the uncritical thinking associated with childhood that we must emulate. Rather, it is the willingness to believe, the Berean eagerness to learn new truth, that is so characteristic of a child.

Along with being "believers," Christ calls His disciples to become "thinkers." Perhaps Christians don't emphasize this fact enough. Paul wrote: "Brothers, don't think like children . . . think like adults" (1 Cor. 14:20). The writer of Proverbs put it this way: "the simple [naive] believes every word, but the wise looks well to his way" (Prov. 14:15). That means that God expects us to have childlike eagerness in learning, but adult discrimination in determining what to believe.

You are not a tape recorder, uncritically recording all you hear. You are not a sponge, soaking up truth and error alike. You must learn to discriminate. Faith is not a leap in the dark; it is not a willingness to believe against all reason. It is not an acceptance of that which is pleasing. It is trust in the Word of God. You must always be open to new ideas, but only as open as a *thorough,* Berean-like study of the Bible permits. Teaching from the pulpit, like teaching on radio or TV, must be carefully *evaluated.* It is only when you can set forth that teaching yourself, together with a plain, biblical rationale for it, that you may be said to "understand" in the sense commended in the Parable of the Sower.

Hard Work

The Berean commendation (Acts 17) indicates that the Bereans worked hard at discovering the truth. *Daily,* they studied the Scriptures to determine whether Paul's preaching was *true.* Augustine says, "To proclaim the Word of truth as well as to listen to it is hard work. . . . Thus, let us exert ourselves in listening."[3] And, as I have been contending in previous chapters, proper listening does not end with the closing words of the sermon but extends to work done after the preaching event. The Bereans were commended for not making a snap judgment about Paul's preaching. They didn't think of accepting his message uncritically—on the spot. The

Bible holds them forth as an example of people who worked hard to evaluate the message according to biblical standards. *That* is listening—biblical listening—*par excellence.*

The main problem with this is the laziness and lack of discipline among pampered Christians. People want truth *instantly,* served up warm, with little or no effort on their part to obtain it. They would prefer to have truth zapped into them at 2 A.M. (while sleeping so that they might not experience any discomfort connected with the transaction) and awaken the next day in full possession of it. But listening, as the Bible everywhere describes it, and as the example of the Bereans plainly indicates, takes time and effort. Are *you* willing to listen that way? Are you willing to discipline yourself to take good notes on sermons, schedule definite times to study what was said in the light of scriptural teaching, and determine whether what was said was true? God holds you responsible to do so.

Do you even own a good Bible dictionary, a concordance, or any commentaries? Do you have a cross-reference Bible? Do you know how to use it? If you are not supplied with such study tools, or if you have them, but don't use them, you can hardly be serious about listening.

How to Evaluate
The following few suggestions may help you in your study.

1. Ask, "Was the questionable statement based on Scripture, or was it simply something the preacher threw in on his own?"

2. Be careful of statements that begin with "I believe ... I think ... " It seems to me ..." What you want is not the opinion of the preacher, but a message from God.

3. Ask, "Was the material complete?" Sermons can say only so much. Are there other angles, qualifications, elsewhere in the Bible? Use your concordance and Bible dictionary.

4. Ask, "Did I really understand him?" If you are hazy

about any important point, ask someone else who was there to clarify. Or, if all else fails, call the pastor and ask him about it (but don't drive him up a tree doing this every week).

These are but a few suggestions to get you started.

Let's take an example.

You are listening to a sermon on joy from the Book of Philippians. At one point, the preacher says, "You can't love God unless you first fear Him." The sentence strikes you as significant, if true. It is also interesting because of the unusual juxtaposition of "love" and "fear," two words that, to many seem antithetical, rather than complementary. But, the preacher fails to elaborate on his statement. He just leaves it hanging. You write it down. Later, at home, you ponder it and do a study of the two words, using your concordance. As a result, you not only confirm the statement as true, but you begin to get some insight into the relationship of fear to love. For instance, you write down in your loose-leaf notebook: "A person cannot fully know the joy of forgiveness until he has experienced the fear of hell."

Further on in the same sermon, these other words also intrigue you: If you don't learn to fear your parents, the state, etc., you'll never learn to fear God." You make a note of this also. Something about it seems wrong. Should a child's salvation depend so heavily on his parents, that he may never be saved unless taught to fear? The statement seems highly questionable. You note, also, that the preacher offered no biblical support. At home, after a diligent search, you can find nothing in the Bible to support the contention. Indeed, you finally conclude that the Bible teaches the opposite (which you write down in your loose-leaf notebook, along with notes of your study): "The fear of God is what leads to respect for authority elsewhere."

In two ways, therefore, both positively and negatively, the sermon has helped you think through biblical truth. But without further biblical research, what was said in the sermon possibly would have remained as little more than hazy questions in your mind that would fade with time. Having researched them on your own, has not only cleared the haze, but also made the biblical truths far more memorable (you remember more readily that which you carve out for yourself).

Disagreement

In the example previously cited, your own studies led you to think the second statement was wrong; indeed, you concluded the opposite of the statement was true. What should you do about such disagreements? Well, if a pastor's discussion class follows the sermon or is held next week during the Sunday School hour (which is much better because it allows for time to study matters on one's own), you can bring up your questions and the conclusions of your studies. It is possible that your study could use some modification, that you may have misunderstood.

Augustine spoke about misunderstanding when he said, "Now, pay attention; otherwise if you misunderstand you will fling yourselves into that whirlpool of thinking where you may sin with impunity." He goes on to mention a second sort of misunderstanding that is more willful than careless: "They willfully misunderstood ... to act aright you must have the will to understand, then you will arrive at a clear understanding."[4]

Always be open to explanations or help that the pastor may offer. Don't stubbornly cling to your ideas. But, be sure that he convinces you to exchange yours for his only because, after full consideration, you believe his ideas are more scriptural. It is possible, of course, that your study may help the pastor think through his interpretation of Scripture more fully.

If there is no such class for discussion (you might suggest that one be started) you may do one of two things:

1. Drop the matter if it doesn't seem the difference is important enough to mention (you can't raise every issue; learn to choose on the basis of priority).

2. Speak privately with the pastor about the issue. In a

sermon, Augustine once told any members of his congregation who didn't get what he had said that "If they want to question me further on any point, they will find my ear ready to listen to them for Christ's sake."[5] Any faithful pastor would say the same to any reasonable member. But, remember, in a world of sin, Christians will always differ because no one is perfect and no one's knowledge of Scripture is perfect.

In conclusion, it is important to recognize your own position as a Berean-like listener. As the window keeps out wind and rain and dirt, but lets light and heat in, so too, you must admit only the truth of God into your mind. Screen out all else through the filter of Scripture. Truth, and truth alone, enlightens.

CHAPTER TEN

Distractions

Please listen to me—you are not paying attention. I am talking to you about the Holy Scriptures, and you are looking at the lamps and the people lighting them. It is very frivolous to be more interested in what the lamp-lighters are doing. . . . After all, I am lighting a lamp too—the lamp of God's Word.[1]

These words of Chrysostom (A.D. 347–407), taken from his fourth homily on Genesis, show quite clearly that the problem of distraction is nothing new. Like the poor, I suppose, it will always be with us. Preachers—and serious listeners—have always contended with distraction. In his *Screwtape Letters*, C.S. Lewis pictures the demon making hay over the phenomenon:

You want to lean pretty heavily on those neighbors. Make his mind flit to and fro between an expression like "the body of Christ" and the actual faces in the next pew.[2]

Carole Thomas, a layperson, puts it this way:

What in fact occurs is this. Eldest son immediately begins a discussion with dad, usually on a topic related to sending a space probe to various parts of the universe. Younger brother climbs onto father's lap in hopes of gaining paternal attention; this failing, he uses the nearest available hymnal to entertain himself by elaborately bending and folding its pages. My time is about evenly divided in trying to listen to what is being said by the preacher, mentally cursing the whispers beside me, avoiding the glances of the distracted unfortunates sitting in the rows closest to us, and glaring at my beloveds. Occasionally, my glares hit target: conversation ceases, and I can tend to the conversation from the pulpit.

I still can't concentrate. Gradually, I find myself sneaking glances at the progress of the origami beside me, wondering where Mrs. Y bought that gorgeous sweater, trying to think up a good excuse for not going to McDonald's today for lunch, and mentally drafting articles such as this one. Guiltily, I remember where I am, and return to my efforts to listen to the message being preached. Sadly, I often find it not worth the effort.[3]

There is certainly an ability—highly cultivated by the average church member—to tune out the "boring bits."[4]

Scientifically, this God-given ability is due to a conjunction of nerves called (from its shape) the *reticular formation*. This rectangular "junction box" is capable of routing stimuli (including those sounds that emanate from pulpits) away from the brain. The frontal lobes direct the reticular activating system to enhance or diminish the level of excitement of various portions of the cerebral cortex. In short, it is this system that makes "tuning out" possible.

For over a half hour I sat on a bench in Disneyland near the building that houses the "Small World" exhibit. During my wait, the tune "It's a Small World," sounded forth loudly over and over again. The only variation was that Mexican, Italian, Hawaiian, German, and other national renderings of the song were repeated in an endless cycle. At first, it was quite annoying. I couldn't leave, because I had promised to meet my wife and children here. I was stuck. But after a while, I realized that I was no longer being annoyed. My mind had strayed to something else, and I had simply tuned out the music. I didn't "hear" it. That is to say, the reticular formation dampened it so that the sound didn't register. People who live near waterfalls or railways soon learn not to hear. Of course, nothing in the outside world has changed; only something in the individual. That is the phenomenon we must discuss in this chapter.

The problem has several dimensions. Not only do we learn to "tune out" those things that trouble or bore us, but we also learn to switch our attention to those that seem more interesting. Distraction is that shift from the former to the latter. It is that to which Chrysostom referred when noticing his congregation's attention shifting from the sermon to the lamplighters. He was right in raising the question about which was more important to his congregation.

Fundamentally, there are two sources of distraction: those outside and those within the individual. A distraction must not be conceived as a mere interruption from without. We distract ourselves by allowing our mind to drift and by consciously changing channels.

Even when interruptions from without (like the lamplighters) are the original source of the distraction, if we allow ourselves more than a moment's shift from the sermon and concentrate instead on the new occurence, we are responsible for the more permanent shift of attention that follows. In the final analysis, *you* are your own biggest distraction.

Environmental Distractions

You may allow almost anything to distract you—especially if you are uninterested in what the preacher is saying. Clocks, wrongly placed, so that everyone may see them, may be a prime cause of distraction: some will "time" the message rather than listen to it. The temperature (too hot or too cold) can also become more important than a word from God. Some people look at plaster cracks and paint peelings, while others count the organ pipes. Another favorite distraction is the folds in the drape behind the pulpit—are there the same number as last week?

While writing this chapter, *The Associate Presbyterian Magazine* for November 1989 crossed my desk. In it was an altogether appropriate cartoon. The first box showed a preacher and his son. The son is speaking:

"Well . . . there are 4,314 acoustical tiles on the ceiling. At 144 holes per tile that gives us 621,216 holes."

In box two, the preacher is walking off dejectedly, saying to himself, "Never ask your own kid how he liked your sermon."

Some buildings are shaped in circles or semicircles, so that one-third of the congregation faces another third. Naturally, this arrangement invites people to watch others instead of the preacher. Choir watching (and vice versa) is a common distraction for those congregations in which the choir does not process from the loft behind the preacher before the message.

Noisy air conditioners and heating systems are a great distraction for some, especially if they go on and off multiple times during the sermon. Some learn to count the minutes between each new blast of cold or hot air. Public address systems—especially when they squeal, or when the operator fiddles with the volume through the message—are first-rate distracters. In one large church, after years of failure, the same operator, every week, never failed to call attention to the P.A. system by poorly tuning it in—thereby enabling all those who were habituated to do so, to know when to tune the preacher out.

Churches designed with vertical strips (or drape folds) that run directly behind the preacher enable members to more easily drop off to sleep. As the preacher sways back and forth in front of them, he quickly induces a hypnotic trance. Soft lighting, comfortable pews, and similar helps all contribute to the effect.

Now, of course, none of these things need distract you *if you refuse to allow them.* Churches may minimize obvious environmental distractions, but distractions will always be left to provide adequate stimulation for those looking to shift their attention. And creativity, at this level, seems limitless. The final decision about whether you will attend to the sermon lies with you. And it is nothing less than that—a decision.

The reticular formation is a blessing from God that, like all good things, has been perverted. Consciously attending to every sound in the environment at all times would soon overload your nervous system. You could not do so for an hour. That is why the nervous system allows you to choose among sounds. This selectivity determines what will register and what will not. But combined with habit (patterns of unconscious decision-making), the capability provided by the reticular activating system can be used for ill as readily as for good. You can *learn* to *habitually* tune out certain sounds while tuning in others.

It is the nature of a sinner to allow his mind to be diverted from truth, while tuning in to error or matters of no consequence. This problem preeminently manifests itself when a person is praying or listening to sermons. Even biblical preachers found it necessary to urge their congregations to "Listen to what I say." (Acts 2:14 literally says, "Get this in your ear.") When naval officers want to command attention, they announce, "Now hear this!" In order to alter a long-standing habit that is displeasing to God, it may be necessary to command yourself at the beginning of a sermon "Now hear this" or "Get this in your ear!"

Human Distractions
Why do we develop such habits? Not only because we are sinners—that just makes it easy to go wrong. One key reason is because our parents (unwittingly) trained some of us *not* to listen to sermons.

Thinking (wrongly) that it pleases God to drag children into pews before they are capable of understanding the preacher, parents teach their children to sit for 30–40 minutes, *doing something other than* listening to the sermon. Some play with cars, dolls, or other toys. Others draw pictures or fold church bulletins into airplanes and hats. Many sleep (surely one significant cause of sermon sleepiness later on). A good number scream, crawl on the floor or on the pews, thus providing a rich lode of distractions for others nearby. These antics also tend to embarrass or enrage (read "distract") parents as well. Often, children carry on so much that they force parents to leave with them, thus causing further distraction to all. Listen to this:

> As a child in the Netherlands, I used to assess the length—though not the quality—of my father's sermons by a popularly accepted standard. Our pockets (or mother's purse) always contained a white and blue roll of KING peppermints. If my father preached a short sermon, then one or perhaps two mints would suffice. More likely, though, it would take three or four—and a five mint sermon was a lengthy effort indeed! It sometimes troubles me that of all the sermons I heard my father preach, I remember only the peppermints. Though I also remember frequently snuggling into my mother's side and being not strangely warmed and soothed.[5]

Snuggling up to mother is fine for a child. But not for an adult! And many, perhaps most, adults find that in one form or another such childish practices persist. The sermon remains a time to be warmed and soothed, adults allowing their minds to daydream and play over all sorts of things that please and coddle them.

I know that what I am about to say will draw fire. But it must be said anyway, because it is biblical. It is *not* pious to bring children to the exposition of Scripture *until they are able to understand what is said.* In Nehemiah 8:1-8, we read that "all who could understand" were gathered for the reading and the exposition of the Law (vv. 2-3, 8). Others were left at home or, possibly (as some churches wisely do today), dismissed into the care of persons who can teach them something they *can* understand on their own level.

If you refuse your children admittance to the preaching service until such a time as they are old enough to understand the message (no set age is given: some children mature before others), they will not develop poor listening habits, which become ingrained over the years. Moreover, they will not distract others (including their parents) by antics on the pews, or by running to the bathroom. And, perhaps of greatest importance, they will be anxious to "graduate" to that advanced stage where they are allowed to come to the preaching service. They will consider listening a privilege rather than a punishment!

Although I have mentioned several human distractions already (choir watching, congregation watching), I want to note a few more. Clothing surveys ("I wonder why she wore those earrings with that dress?"), are a favorite female pastime. Men, on the other hand, may have difficulty keeping their eyes off attractive women (or their anatomy). And, members of the congregation who preen their hair, smooth their skirts, or adjust their ties throughout the message, make it apparent that their prime concern is the effect they hope to have on others. Clearly, their minds are (at best) only partially focused on what the preacher is saying.

Coming to church with minds loaded down with concerns is another form of self-distraction. Not only should preparations for church be made the day before, but (as I have noted) you should allow plenty of time to travel to church in a leisurely manner. Arguments and problems should be strictly avoided on Sunday morning.

We distract ourselves in many ways. No one could begin to specify all our methods. Indeed, probably each person has his own peculiar set of distractions, in addition to those that seem common to all. These, though I could not deal with them here, may cause the greatest difficulty for serious listeners; therefore, I suggest the following:

● Make a list of all the distractions you face when listening to sermons, noting especially those that are unique to you.

● Take this list with you and prayerfully read it during the prelude asking God to help you combat these distractions.

● At the beginning of the sermon, say to yourself: "Get this in your ear!"

It is important, when possible, to anticipate certain distractions and take action to prevent them. For instance, if children who cannot yet understand the sermon are allowed in the preaching service, and this is a constant distraction for you, be sure to sit in a seat that is as far removed from them as possible. If you find yourself dozing off, in addition to those suggestions given in an earlier chapter, I suggest that you move to the front of the church—perhaps to the first pew. Remember this aphorism: "Sit near . . . and hear." It is easier to avoid distractions when they are behind you, and it is more difficult to snooze when seated directly under the gaze of the preacher. The front pew solution is a good one for solving many listening problems (and, interestingly, the front pew is almost always available, being the last to be occupied).

Refuse to allow your mind to drift. Keep bringing it back to the message. Work on this. Practice doing it week after week until you get control over your mind (as Philippians 4:8-9 requires) and learn good habits of listening. You must learn to discipline your mind.

Taking notes properly sometimes helps; but, as I suggested before, don't take too many notes (record only new or questionable ideas). Prolific note-taking can become an end in itself which, in its own way, also becomes a distraction. I will talk more about note-taking at a later point.

When Beethoven became stone deaf, he learned that by clenching a stick in his teeth he could hold it against a piano sounding board and thus detect sounds. Such a desperate effort to hear! You, who have perfectly good hearing (or excellent hearing devices) must demonstrate every bit as much effort to hear the chords of truth and harmonies of heaven preached from God's own Holy Word!

CHAPTER ELEVEN

The Preacher and You

In discussing the priesthood of all believers, I mentioned that Jesus provided pastor-teachers to assist members of congregations in their tasks of understanding and implementing biblical truth. But I also showed that the need for teachers is not absolute. Each believer has the "Anointing" (the Holy Spirit) whose task is to "teach [him] all things" (See 1 John 2). But, under ordinary circumstances, God-given teachers do meet a real need.

An Enthusiastic Congregation

In this chapter I want to discuss the fact that the preacher also needs the congregation. Obviously, no congregation, no preaching; but that isn't what I have in mind. Full, enthusiastic congregations can mean better preaching. In fact, such congregations encourage preachers to excel. One reason why your preacher may be dull (if, indeed he is) may be that he is reacting to a dull congregation. And one reason why a congregation is dull is because you—and others like you—have been dull listeners.

A congregation, and individual members thereof, can influence preaching in many ways. Empty pews, that ought to be full, can tempt preachers to become so discouraged that they begin to preach "O-what's-the-use?" sermons. Or, on the other hand, they may be tempted to browbeat those who do occupy pews. Chrysostom said he would preach regardless:

> If not everyone listens, half will listen: if not a half, a third; if not a third, a tenth. If even one from the crowd listens, let him hear. It is not a small thing for even one

sheep to be saved, since that shepherd left the ninety-nine sheep and ran after the one that had strayed. I do not despise anyone; even if he is only one, he is a human being...As for me, I will not stop speaking, even if there is no one at all who listens...I am a teacher, I am bidden to give advice...pretexts and excuses are made by careless listeners.[1]

But Chrysostom is an exception. Few preachers have such determination. And, of course, Chrysostom speaks of "crowds"—which were always present and unusually enthusiastic. He never faced the hypothetical situation about which he wrote.

In bad weather, when the pastor was not present, a lay preacher once preached to a small gathering at a service in a country church. Among the worshipers was a young man named C.H. Spurgeon. God used that sermon, though generally miserable in form, content, and delivery to convert Spurgeon, who became one of the world's greatest preachers. Every preacher knows the story; every preacher *knows* that God can do great things among small groups if He wishes. But lean attendance, and diminishing numbers over a period of time provide a great temptation for a preacher to become discouraged.

During the delivery of a message a certain "gelling factor" often occurs. When a preacher has prepared well, and preached extemporaneously (perhaps from an outline), putting together words in sentences as he goes, new ideas and ways of saying things pop into his head. He will find himself saying things that he didn't plan to say. Often, this turns out to be some of the best material in the sermon. Good preachers recognize this and, after preaching, write these thoughts into their sermon notes.

The encouragement of a good congregation (one that is full, receptive, enthusiastic, and prayerful) creates an atmosphere that the Holy Spirit uses to put things together in ways the preacher never intended. In delivery, the sermon is advanced a step beyond the shape it took in the study. What I am saying is that God uses congregations to help preachers better help congregations. Henry Ward Beecher recognized this when he said, "An audience always puts me in possession of everything I have got. There is nothing in the world that is such a stimulus to me. It wakes up the power of thinking and of imagination in me."[2] A good congregation, by egging a preacher on, may do more to help him improve his preaching than anything else. Audible amens, well-placed and not overdone, are not only biblical but encouraging as well.

Maintaining Your Own Enthusiasm

Individual members of the congregation may also help. An encouraging word just before the service ("Pastor, I been looking forward to hearing this sermon all week"), when sincere, can do wonders. When was the last time you said something like that to *your* pastor? If your attitude is right, and you are prepared to use the principles and practices set forth in this book, you can *honestly* say something similar to that statement, even when your pastor's messages, themselves, leave much to be desired.

In an earlier chapter, I talked about recognizing the preacher as a herald who comes with God's message, and urged you to not miss the message for criticizing the messenger. My point there was to encourage you to distinguish the two and to help you remember who sent the message through the messenger. Karl Heim, German homiletician, says:

> It is this fact which so often robs the sermons, preached in our churches, of their power. Just as a truck, too heavily loaded, finds it impossible to climb a hill, so is the Word, which the church speaks concerning God, overburdened by the sinfulness of those who declare it, rendered pointless and ineffectual. The words are robbed of power because they are spoken by sinners. It is not possible to entirely separate a message from the one who presents and advocates it.[3]

He is right, no absolute differentiation can be made. But insofar as it is possible, you must distinguish between the two rather than be put off by the messenger and thus miss God's truth. Something like the separation I am suggesting must have been what Jesus meant when He told His disciples to do as the scribes and Pharisees say but not as they do because they "sit in Moses' seat" (Matt. 23:2-3).

Perhaps the situation extends beyond the mere fact of sermonic ineptness. Perhaps you and your preacher have had a falling out. Your problem is greater than some general dislike for him. For some reason or other, you and he are in an unreconciled condition. He may or may not know of the problem. If he does, he ought to approach you in an attempt to establish proper relations. But, perhaps, through a misunderstanding, he doesn't realize that you have something against him. In either case you must go to him and resolve the matter biblically (Luke 17:3).[4] When God forbids you to let the sun go down on your anger (Eph. 4:26), it is sin to come to church with a chip on your shoulder. And, if you are holding a grudge against another member of the congregation rather than the pastor, this too can contaminate the preaching atmosphere. Such pollution must be cleared away!

But, in passing, let me also mention that when you disagree with something the minister says in his sermon, *don't tell him at the door as you leave.* That is not a personal offense between the two of you, leading to an unreconciled condition. Discussions of disagreements can wait awhile.

When I began teaching preaching at Westminster Theological Seminary in Philadelphia, I found that for years student preaching had been evaluated by faculty *immediately* following the message. In time, I changed this because I discovered that this method not only destroyed a sense of worship for the rest of the class, but it also meant that the preacher would rarely receive any criticism. Instead, I told the preacher to watch the videotape of his message during the week and then one week later, we'd talk about the sermon privately. This worked much better. When a preacher is "up" for his message, bent with every fiber in his body on delivering what he believes to be God's Word, he is in no condition to receive criticism. Chemically, his body is "souped up" for the task. Criticize him immediately after preaching, when he is still wired for preaching, and he *should* be ready to fight for truth. That is why I strongly suggest that you wait until later to make any negative comments about the sermon. You'll get a much better hearing.

In addition, *you* will have time to calm down, think things through, and study the matter. You may change your mind about what the preacher said once you have carefully reflected on it. You may decide that the point on which you disagree isn't that important after all. At least you will approach the pastor in a better frame of mind if you take time to cool off.

This discussion raises another matter: watch out for your buttons. A preacher (or anyone else) can push any number of those buttons with impunity—you may differ about those matters, but you will do so (if you make a point of it at all) lovingly, almost academically. But, just let him hit one or two buttons that are painted red and you explode. Disconnect the wires to these buttons when you go to church.

One of the most reasonable, scholarly, pleasant, and calm persons I have known—a professor of some stature—had three buttons that you didn't dare lay a finger on: eschatology, Christian liberty, and separation. I happened to push the first, and he never let me forget it. He hounded me for years about it. Don't take it out on your preacher if, in preaching the whole counsel of God, he touches on certain areas about which you are supersensitive. Instead, you must get control of yourself; the problem is yours, not his.

Along this line is your response to certain emotion-laden terms. All you have to do is mention some words (*amillenialism, inerrancy, predestination*) to set some people off. Become aware of those words and phrases that you permit to "make you see red," and learn to cool it when you hear them. Some become so emotionally upset that they read into what the preacher is saying ideas he never intended to convey. At any rate, if you don't develop the fruit of self-control, you will never be able to learn from a preacher anything new in these areas.

In short, *from your side,* you must be sure to do all you can to maintain a good relationship with your preacher (see Romans 12:18) and learn not to allow interpersonal problems of any sort to get in the way of fruitful listening, thereby robbing you of truth from God.

Prayer

The Bible makes it clear that you should pray for your preacher—especially regarding his preaching. In Ephesians 6:19-20, Paul writes:

> And pray for me that I may be given the right words to say when I open my mouth, to make known the secret of the Good News boldly (for I am an ambassador with a chain) that I may speak boldly, as indeed I should.

And in Colossians 4:3-4, Paul writes:

> praying at the same time also about us, that God may open for us a door for the Word, to speak about the secret of Christ, because of which I am in bonds, so that I may proclaim it clearly, as I ought to.

These are remarkable requests in light of the fact that the Holy Spirit promised to give the Apostles not only the right content, but the proper words in which to deliver it (see Matthew 10:19-20; Mark 13:11; Luke 12:11-12; 21:14-15). Presumably He did so in response to the prayers of the saints, not apart from human agency. That is why Paul asked these churches to pray that he would preach clearly and boldly and that he would do so in the right words. Surely, if the Apostle Paul needed prayer for his preaching, your pastor does too—no matter how good he is!

Pray as a family for the preacher. Pray for his preparation during the week. Pray for the delivery of the sermon on Sunday. And, pray for the congregation's (including your own) reception of it.

> In 1872 Mr. Moody went to London to rest. While resting, he was over-persuaded to preach for one Sabbath. The place seemed cold and dead, and Mr. Moody himself only half up to the mark. But, while preaching he suddenly awoke to find the atmosphere charged with the Spirit of God . . . a work of grace began then and there. Hundreds were brought to the church.
>
> What was the secret of all this? A friend tells it: "There were two sisters belonging to that church, one strong and the other bedridden. One day as the sick woman was bemoaning her condition, the thought came to her that she could pray, and she did begin to pray that God would revive the church, but the church remained dead and cold. Reading of Mr. Moody's meetings in America, she asked God to send him some day to her church. When her sister returned home from the morning service, she said: 'Who do you think preached for us today? Mr. Moody from America.' The invalid turned pale and said, 'I know that means God has answered my prayer.' All that afternoon she fasted and prayed, and with the evening service came the answer in fire from heaven."
>
> Perhaps few in London knew the woman even existed; but God knew, and in answer to her prayer, brought a Pentecost to that church."[5]

There are many such accounts. A number show that once a congregation, or certain members of it, begin to pray fervently for their preacher, his preaching not only improves, but revival comes.

In his second discourse on Psalm 31, Augustine told his congregation:

To begin with, I commend my inability to your prayers, *that speech may be given me,* as the Apostle says, *that I may open my mouth,* and address you in such a way that speaking may hold no peril for me, and hearing may be salutary for you.[6]

But remember, when you pray for clarity in sermons, *expect* it. Expect not only your preacher's teaching to become easier to understand, but that the clarity with which he speaks will touch sin in your life more plainly than ever before and will convict you. Expect challenges from Scripture that you once could avoid because they were unclear to become inescapably plain. But, precious promises also should gleam with a new brightness.

Remember too, that when you pray for boldness, the answer to that prayer means your preacher will be talking with a new freedom about matters from which he shied away before. He will begin to "meddle." He will become fearlessly specific about sins, will speak more directly, and will not mince words. He will say hard things that you may not want to hear.

Some people may become angry in answer to your prayers; others may leave. Some may even slander or persecute the preacher. In the Scriptures, that's what happened to preachers who were clear and bold. Stick by him and keep praying! Faithful, praying listeners will grow under such preaching. Indeed, that revival you thought could never come to *your* congregation may indeed sweep through your body of believers.

The upshot of what I have been saying is that you have a crucial part to play in the preaching ministry of your church. Don't fail your preacher, the rest of the congregation, yourself or, most of all—the Lord!

CHAPTER TWELVE

Implementation

Virtually everything said so far is worthless apart from implementation. It is wonderful to know *what* to do, but if you never get around to doing what God says, what good will your knowledge do you? This is precisely what James meant when he said, "Faith without works is dead" (James 2:17). He graphically pictures the same idea when he writes about those who look into the mirror of God's Word, then turn away, forgetting the sins and inadequacies they saw just like when we forget the smudges on our face when we turn from the mirror (James 1:23-25).

Hearing That Honors God
Perhaps the verse from James on the *back* of a church sign, greeting worshipers as they left the church building, says it all: BE DOERS OF THE WORD AND NOT HEARERS ONLY (James 1:22). As a man rose from the pew one Sunday morning, he said, "Well, the sermon is over." Another replied, "No, now is when it begins!" Hearing, of the sort that honors God and is blessed by Him, is hearing in the sense of *heeding.*[1]

Hearing is worthless apart from obedience. An old proverb puts it this way:

I hear and I forget
I see and I remember
I do and I understand

According to that proverb, until one *does* the will of God, he does not really "understand." That is precisely the kind of understanding Jesus was talking about in the Parable of the Sower, when He spoke of those who understand *and bear fruit.*

In a real sense, obedience is what the Bible means by "hearing." Note the following verses from Jeremiah:

• "We have not obeyed the voice of the Lord!" (Jer. 3:2-5) When God speaks, He expects to be heard in the sense of obeyed.

• "You shall speak . . . but they will not listen" (Jer. 7:27). God sends His prophet with a word to be *obeyed;* His people will not "listen." That is, they will not pay attention to Him; they will not obey His commands.

• "But if they will not listen. . . . If you listen attentively" (Jer. 12:17; 17:23-24, 25, 27). To listen attentively is to listen with intent to do.

• In this verse the people's failure to listen provokes God to anger (Jer. 25:7; see N.B. also 26:3-6).

Again and again, throughout the Old Testament, the problem God's servants face is getting a hearing for God's message, a hearing that brings about change. I have almost casually dipped into Jeremiah to show how the theme runs through that book. But what Jeremiah says could be replicated throughout the prophets. As James indicates, to get people to heed God's Word is also a New Testament problem.

Why We Don't Heed the Word

Now, there are various reasons for this failure. First, as we noted at the outset, unbelievers cannot please God (Rom. 8:8). They "hear," but do not hear (Matt. 15:8). The reason why some church members do not obey God's voice is, surely, because their profession of faith is spurious. Too many today have been admitted into membership who have no right to it. In many cases, this is the fault of the church and stems from an inordinate concern for church growth. In other cases, even where care has been taken to screen out false professions, errors have been made because officers of the church cannot read another's heart. This cannot be helped. Jesus

Himself told us that "tares" would grow together with the wheat until the harvest.

A second reason why the Word of God is not heeded is because the believer wants to continue the practice of certain sinful habits. I have already said enough about this problem throughout the book.

I want to concentrate on the third reason why believers ignore God's Word. Many Christians do not obey the voice of the Lord *because they do not know how to.*

At conversion they experienced the deep sense of gratitude called the "first love" (Rev. 2:4), which gave them a burning desire to please the Lord by doing whatever He required. They were zealous and highly motivated. Hearing a message urging them to do such and such, they went out fired up to obey. But because they did not know *how* to begin or how to take the first step when they tried—they failed! They fell flat on their faces.

Later, trying again, again they failed. Over and over the same thing happened—all because they were clearly told *what* to do, but they were given no instruction about how to pull if off. Eventually they gave up saying, "Well, maybe Paul could do it; but I'm not Paul!" Then they went to sleep in the pews.

Beecher spoke of this problem, although he probably did not quite understand the dynamic behind it:

> So there are thousands and thousands of persons in the church who hear the doctrine of purity, and the doctrine of self-sacrifice; and, while they are here, they are not only in sympathy with these things, but they say, "God do so to me, and more also, if from this hour I do not try to practice this." Nevertheless, the door is hardly closed upon them in their own houses, and the opportunity scarcely presents itself of putting them in practice among their servants, and children, and friends, and acquaintances, before the impulse is gone,
>
> "In honor preferring one another."

We are coming down the Ohio. There is a pleasant company of some two-score persons. They know that I am on board, and they come to me with the request, "Will you give us a Sunday morning talk?" and it is arranged, and I preach to them, in my way—I talk to them, taking for my text this passage: "In honor preferring one another." I show them how beautiful it is. I illustrate it. I show them how beautiful it is to prefer those that are inferior. I tell them how grand and noble a man feels who treats his servants, the lowest of them, with a consideration which makes them more manly. I can see one and another drop a tear, or wipe it away; and so I go on, opening up the beauty of disinterestedness and of studying one another's happiness. I keep talking to them in this strain until I perceive that dinner is ready to be served, and I give out a hymn, and it is sung, and I close the meeting. Then the gong sounds,— and every man tears for that dinner door; every man rushes for the table, pulling and hauling and trying to get the best place, opposite the choicest dish; and everybody goes to eating with all his might, and nobody waits on anybody. And when they have gorged themselves, they begin to wipe their faces, and say, "We had a good sermon this morning." At the very first opportunity they had of carrying out the principle, their old nature, their old life, their old basilar habits, prevailed.[2]

Bible-believing preachers have excelled in telling their members what to do but have been sadly remiss in spelling out the how-to. Consequently, many fail and fail again and then give up. Has that been one of your problems, Christian? Well, you shouldn't give up. You should persevere until you discover how: by asking others, talking to your preacher, reading up on the matter, etc. Galatians 6:9 reminds us: "And don't get tired of doing good; at the right time we shall reap if we don't slacken." Perseverance is difficult enough when you do know how, as this verse indicates. We tend to give up (or slacken in effort) when immediate results are not forthcoming. That is what Paul is saying to the Galatians. But Colossians 3:24 deals with that: even if others give up, ultimately, your Lord will say, "Well done, you good and faithful servant." It is Christ that we serve. But if those who are succeeding can slacken their efforts and even give up, how much easier is it for those who have never succeeded to do so? It is that failure that comes from not knowing how to implement biblical commands we are considering here.

Understanding Implementation
Let's try to understand implementation. First, implementation involves careful and accurate understanding of the biblical command. If this is not right, all else is sure to fail. A number of people fail right here. They settle for vague notions of the Lord's will. Either they listen poorly, or the preacher fails to communicate well, or both. Either way, it is the fault of the listener, if he doesn't make an effort to clear up any fuzziness about the command. If you don't understand what God wants you to do, ask, study, and work at coming to that full knowledge of God's will. Nothing less will do. That again is the essence of the Berean spirit that the Bible commends.

Secondly, it is necessary to determine whether there is biblical how-to attached to the command. If so, you should have little difficulty in implementing it. Throughout the Sermon on the Mount, for instance, you are told not only *what* to do but also how *to* do it and how *not* to do it. This is true of the commands to pray, give alms, fast, etc.

More frequently, however, God commands you to do something, but does not tell you exactly how to carry out the command. That means He assumes you will use the mind He gave you to figure out the best way to implement the command. You are free, in such cases, to follow various suggestions or come up with your own, as you like, so long as the implementation grows out of and is consistent with general biblical principles. If you are not sure about the correctness of a possible course of action, run it past an elder or two in your church. That is one reason why God gave officers to His church. Part of our growth as Christians is learning how to use general scriptural principles to develop ways and means for obeying God. Those who learn to do so, show signs of spiritual growth. Get help, when you need it, but also work at it on your own (see Philippians 2:12-13).

Thirdly, implementation often involves planning. Plan what to do, where, and when (i.e. schedule it). You may want to break your action up into steps: "First, I must phone Jan and set up an appointment. Then, I must speak to her about the problem that came between us. Lastly, assuming reconciliation takes place, I must develop a new relationship with her (which also will take planning)."

Along the way questions will arise: "When would it be best to talk to Joan? Probably over lunch, to which I shall invite her, and for which I shall pay. Which restaurant would be the best? How shall I begin the conversation?" All of this is important. Paul wrote: "Plan ahead to do what is fine in the eyes of every one" (Rom. 12:17). The word *fine* indicates that we should make an effort to do good, not perfunctorily, but with concern. A fine dinner takes much previous planning. Anyone can open a can of beans and set it on the table! God wants you to plan to obey *with care.* He expects you to do it the best way: implementation with finesse!

Again, if you need help, get it. Let me emphasize one more thing: the best plans, if unscheduled, will probably fizzle if indeed they are ever carried out. Assign yourself a date for every step, then keep on schedule. Unless you actually get around to implementing the plan by acting on it, your best intentions are worthless.

As you can see, implementation may fail at any number of spots. Why not run through the stages of implementation again, noting where you generally have the greatest problems? Having done so, make a special effort to overcome these difficulties, asking God (and possibly a Christian friend) to help.

Note Taking

One helpful device for implementing truth is proper note taking. Notes, carried home, help you remember that you received a message from God that should make a difference in the way you live this week. They also provide a place to begin planning your implementation.

Some notes should be entered into the margin of your Bible. These notes should consist largely of explanatory material, important cross references, and whatever else will help you to remember what was said *about the text.* Notes taken on the church bulletin (and later transcribed at home into your notebook), or on a small pad or notebook, should have to do with *what was said about you.* The first we could call expository notes; the second, applicatory notes.

Too many Christians take only expository notes. That is one reason why they fail to implement biblical commands. Having taken profuse notes (a mistake) on what the passage says, they think they have achieved a great deal. There are people who bring notebooks and write down everything the preacher says. When they get home, they simply shelve the notebook. The problem with this method is that when they shelve the notebook, they also shelve the sermon—commands and all.

Rather, you should take few expository notes. That is one reason for writing them in the margin of the Bible itself. Another is, of course, so that any future reading of the text will be illumined by the notes.

Another poor practice is outlining the sermon. Why do it? What's the purpose? If you follow this practice long enough, you'll become proficient at outlining. What God wants is for you to become proficient at living the truths of His word.

Focus your notes, therefore, on *what* God is telling you to to believe, disbelieve, do, or not do. Listen for commands—jot them down, as I have shown you before. You might even consider taking a sheet of the following applicatory questions with you to keep your thinking on track. Fill in the answers and post the sheet on the refrigerator door:

1. How does God want me to change (beliefs/actions)?

2. How must I bring about the change?

3. What is the first step?

4. Where and when should I begin?

I could say a great deal more about implementation, but I want you to begin the task and not become overwhelmed with things to do. If you follow the simple, basic, and important suggestions in this chapter, you will learn for yourself many more sophisticated things to do in the future. You must begin somewhere—that is the whole point of implementation. And there is plenty here for you to begin doing. Will you?

God, Your Neighbor, and You

Because I have placed so great an emphasis on how to get the most out of preaching—a very legitimate concern—you might think this book is a call to self-centeredness. As I said in my book on Christian education, *Back to the Blackboard,* all truth must be learned for life and ministry. That means it is wrong indeed, idolatrous, to learn truth "for truth's sake." Nothing for the Christian can exist for its own sake; all must exist for God's glory. That's why shelved notebooks or heads full of unused information are sinful. That is why, at this strategic point, just before concluding, I want to take the time to consider listening for life and for ministry.

The Two Commandments

Jesus was perfectly clear when He summarized the teachings of the Bible (Matt. 22:37-40). He said that everything in the Bible could be hung on two commandments (v. 40). These two firm pegs are:

1. To love God with all your being;
2. To love your neighbor as yourself.

It shouldn't be necessary to point out that these two commandments point away from self to God and others. But, in a day when humanistic thinking undergirds society and has permeated the church in the form of self-esteem teaching, I must now make a point of what used to be perfectly obvious.

In order to find some biblical basis for their views (there is none), self-image promoters in the church have seized on the second commandment: "Love your neighbor as yourself."

"See," they say, "you must also love yourself. Here is a command, more basic than the first two, because they are based upon it. You cannot love God or others until you first learn to love yourself."[1]

But, the attempt to construe Jesus' words that way only reveals how desperate the effort to find biblical support for such unscriptural teachings is. First, note well that Jesus says nothing of a third commandment. He is speaking only of two. He talks about the "first" (v. 38) and the "second" (v. 39). Moreover, His final summary statement is "On those *two* commandments hang all the Law and the Prophets." Where is the third, supposedly more basic, command? It simply isn't there.

Notice, also, not only is there no third commandment more basic than the others, but Jesus *presupposes* that we already love ourselves far too much (as does Paul in Romans 12:3) when He commands us to love others "as ourselves" (literally, in accordance with) the love we *already* have for ourselves. What does He mean by that? The words *as ourselves* do not mean that we should do for others the same things that we do for ourselves. Our self-concerns could never be the standard for our conduct toward others. Why, we do all sorts of sinful, harmful things to ourselves that Jesus would certainly not want us to do to another person. That isn't what those two words mean at all; the standard of our conduct toward others is the Scriptures.

When comparing the second love commandment to the first, Jesus says, "The second is just like it" (v. 39). In what way? Well, surely not only in the sense that both commands deal with love—that is too patent for Him to make a point of it. But, what is similar is *the way in which love must be shown.* Love for God is to be wholehearted: "With all your heart and with all your soul and with all your mind" (v. 37). So, likewise, love for a neighbor should be as intense, as deep, and as wide-ranging as the love you already show to yourself. It is not the content of self-love Jesus is urging you to show another, but the vigor of self-love.

So, it is clear that in getting the most out of a sermon you are not to think of what you can learn in a self-centered way; instead, you are to learn all you can to please and honor God and to be a blessing to others.

Other-directed Love and Learning

Sadly, our Christian schools often foster self-centered learning. They are often close copies of pagan schools down the block largely because Christians didn't take the time to think through what they were doing when they started the Christian school movement. They hurried ahead, on false assumptions, adopting presuppositions that did not stem from biblical exegesis. Perhaps the most glaring—one that has caused much difficulty—is an adoption of the humanistic principle that a child must be educated *for his benefit.* Such education is essentially selfish. It fails to look beyond the individual to God and others. It idolatrously makes the child himself the end of education. There is talk about doing math "to the glory of God," but little or no practice.

It is clear from Christ's summary of the Bible's purpose that God (ultimately) and others (secondarily) should be the object of what we are and do. They, not ourselves, must be the object of our love. So in listening to preaching, what you get out of the message should be oriented toward how you may better love God and serve your neighbor.

Where do we come into the picture? We do benefit, but only as a by-product. Jesus said this when He told us to seek first the kingdom of God and His righteousness and then (as a by-product) "things" would be "added" to us (Matt. 6:33).

Love that the Bible commands is not self-directed, but other-directed. Self-centered love is condemned (In 2 Timothy 3:2 the item that heads the list, and, in the minds of some interpreters is the one from which all the rest flow, is self-love). Self-love is really lust, which is concerned with *getting.* God's love after which ours must be patterned, is characterized by *giving.* God so loved the world that He GAVE.... He loved me and GAVE.... love your wives as

Christ loved the church and GAVE.... Love your
enemies.... if your enemy hungers (thirsts) GIVE.... and
so it goes.

So, I want you to understand plainly that everything recommended in this book that will benefit you must be done,
not for your benefit (that is a by-product) but *to enable you* to
love God and your neighbor as He commands you. You will
benefit immensely when you learn to listen properly. But that
is secondary. Learn to get the most out of a sermon in order
that you may give the most possible to God and others; that's
the biblical way.

If you expend your efforts solely, or even primarily to gain
advantage for yourself, it might not matter so much whether
you get all you can from preaching. But, when the honor of
God and the welfare of other Christians is at stake, the impe-
tus must be stronger. People who attend church merely for
what they can get out of it for themselves, will always be
disappointed. Self-centeredness always leads to a letdown.
God so constructed human beings that lasting satisfaction
comes only when we look outside ourselves and put others
first. Even Jesus, who was true Man and knew this from
personal experience, functioned that way. It was when He
"saw His seed" that He was "satisfied" (Isa. 53:11; cf. also,
John 4:32).

Listening to sermons out of love, out of concern to know
all you can to please God and help others, is the only proper
and satisfying way to approach preaching. Listening out of
love, makes listening exciting, worthwhile. You must never
lean to one side as a missive from the pulpit is hurled in your
direction, so that it will strike only those seated behind. That
isn't what I am talking about. You must feel the full force of
the blow if it is appropriate for you—in order to change in
ways that will please God and benefit your neighbor. Listening for a neighbor's sake must not be understood as saying,
"Well, pastor, you really told them this morning!"

The person motivated by love of the sort Jesus described
will listen intently, and eagerly, with dedication. He will pur-

sue truth, and its incorporation into daily living, with a vengeance! He will not drag his feet but will enthusiastically engage in the practices recommended in this book. He will become a "noble" Berean. In short, learning out of love for God and others is the only way to go about getting the most out of preaching. Until you make this your motive, don't even attempt to do the things set forth in the previous chapters. They are too strenuous and exacting to follow from any lesser motive. But love will drive you to even more vigorous efforts.

Listening to Please God

First and foremost (the greatest commandment), is listening out of love for God. Pleasing and honoring Him ought to impel you to hear all you can of His Word in order to learn more of Him (to better worship and adore Him) and of His will (to better serve Him).

When you go to church, if it is God's Word you want to hear, preaching should be the event of the week! To the extent that the Scriptures are faithfully preached, God will speak to you. Of course, you may learn God's will by reading the Bible. But reading does not supplant "the foolishness of preaching," by which the Holy Spirit has determined to work. Consider the possibility that the preacher will impart biblical knowledge, and make applications of it, that you might never have garnered on your own. You will also benefit from the challenge and directness of the Word, properly preached, that comes from a messenger who authoritatively proclaims it to you. Preaching may be supplemented by many good things (Bible study, group discussion, lectures), but it must never be supplanted by them.

It is Christ, speaking by His messenger, that you go to church to hear. I have said this before, but here I want to emphasize it: you will *want* to hear Him if you love Him. And when you hear Him, you will want to heed His Word. Listening to One you love should not be irksome, but delightful. True, Christ's voice may be heard in stammering tongue, partially presented and possibly distorted by the messenger. But, if you love Him, and want to know what He is saying, you will make every effort to do so—even under less-than-perfect conditions.

Listening to Help Others

In serving God, we are bid to serve others. It is He who tells us, contrary to self-esteem doctrine, to put others' concerns before our own (see Phil. 2:3-4).

If you are not concerned to listen in order to benefit yourself, realize that as one member of the body, the rest depend on you. You have obligations toward them. You are not on your own.

In Galatians 6:1-5, for instance, you are told to restore those who are caught in some sin from which they are not able to extract themselves. Paul tells you to do so in an attitude of meekness and to avoid falling into temptation yourself while helping others. You must do this in order to bear the burdens of others, thereby fulfilling the Law of Christ (which, as we have seen, is love for others; see Gal. 5:14). But, to restore others in the way Christ commands, takes good judgment. You must bear another's load only insofar as it is necessary to restore him so he can once more carry his own load (v. 5). Otherwise, you will not restore him to his place of responsibility in the church.

All such activities require considerable knowledge and wisdom, much of which the average Christian, studying on his own, will not acquire very quickly. Must others wait until you can bone up on your responsibilities? No, the preaching of the Word makes available the knowledge and directions you need long before you must use them. It speeds growth, develops wisdom, and encourages service.

Preaching challenges us to study, as personal study may not, and it leads us into territory we would never explore if left to ourselves. In Hebrews 10:24-25 the writer tells us not to forsake the assembling of ourselves to hear the Word because doing so provides opportunity to encourage one another to the love and good works taught from the pulpit.

On every count, then, if you listen in love (for God and others) you will "grow by the help [grace] and knowledge of our Lord and Saviour, Jesus Christ," help that is imparted largely by the proclamation of the Word.

CHAPTER FOURTEEN

Technical Matters

When listening to a sermon, you would be helped by knowing something of the elements that form the whole. In this chapter, I want to acquaint you with them.

You take your automobile to the garage. Let's suppose an excellent mechanic works at that garage (too wild a supposition?) You explain a few symptoms. He lifts the hood, moves deliberately to one item, fiddles with it for a moment, and declares: "Well, there's your problem!"

How did he do that? You know little or nothing about automobiles and what you see under the hood looks to you like a jumbled mess! No wonder his proficiency impresses you. You see only what appears to be one tangled whole; he sees parts of various systems and knows which elements of each cause which problems.

The person in the pew receives a sermon as a whole; however, homileticians (sermon mechanics, if you will) know that a sermon is also composed of various elements in several systems. By listening to certain "systems," they too are able to put their finger on a problem (or problems) that may make a sermon ineffective.

Now, it isn't necessary for you to become an expert in determining what is wrong in sermons. But it *is* helpful to understand the systems and some parts of each so that in listening you may be able to know what has gone wrong, and thereby be able to distinguish what is useful from what is not.

The Systems of a Sermon
I am going to give you a mnemonic device that will help you remember each of the vital elements to consider. It is *COLD*

SOAP. The acronym *COLD* stands for the four systems at work in a sermon: *Content, Organization, Language,* and *Delivery* (use of voice and body). *SOAP* reminds you of other elements in the sermon that will interact with each of these systems: *Speaker, Occasion, Audience,* and *Purpose.* The interrelationships are easily seen by placing these acronymns along two sides of a grid:

	C	O	L	D
S				
O				
A				
P				

When each is in proper relationship to the others, a sermon is usually effective. The proper purpose for a specific occasion, for instance, is important. If San Francisco has been devastated by an earthquake, and for three days the media have been talking of little else, when you go to church you want your pastor to tell you God's perspective on this event. If he ignores it entirely, and preaches instead about the Amalekites, you will probably hear little that he says because your mind is full of the earthquake. His purpose and yours do not meet.

Take another example from the grid: *speaker* and *content.* Remember C.S. Lewis' problem—being turned off by the preacher's home life? Well, it was a clash between the *content* (in and of itself worthwhile) and the life of the *speaker* (which Lewis and Company allowed to interfere with the message).

One more example: *language* and *audience.* Formal language fits a morning worship service, but not a junior high hot dog roast. On the other hand, the more relaxed language in a message to youth will hardly be appropriate for a funeral service.

Incidentally, both COLD and SOAP may also be run through interrelational grids of their own:

	C	O	L	D
C				
O				
L				
D				

	S	O	A	P
S				
O				
A				
P				

Again, you can see how this helps you study various aspects of a sermon. *Content* may require some specific *language* which may or may not be used, or used properly. Moving to the next grid, it should be easy to see that the *speaker* chosen for a particular *occasion* (e.g., a missionary rally and a *speaker* who knows little of missions) may or may not have been the appropriate choice. As an exercise to familiarize you with this method of sermon analysis, work out the rest of the boxes in the grids for yourself, trying to cite an instance (real or imagined) when the relationship failed and at least one instance when it succeeded.

Benefits of System Analysis

"This is all interesting," you say, "but of what value is it for my listening?"

To know and use this system of analysis will do at least two things for you. First, it will make you much more aware of all that goes into preaching, causing you to appreciate the many areas in which something can go wrong. That, in itself, should be a valuable lesson for any and every listener. Preaching is not the simple things that many of its severest critics think. Even analyzing a sermon can be complex.

But, secondly, when you are able to pinpoint the source of a problem, often you will find it easier not only to ignore that and focus on more important matters, but also to remedy the difficulty in your own supplementary study when necessary.

Let's explore both of these benefits. If, for example, a preacher's *language* leaves something to be desired, you may learn to ignore that while *concentrating* on *content*. You'll not even need to remedy the difficulty in subsequent personal study (though you may want to encourage the preacher to work on the problem). However, if the interpretation of a passage (biblical *content*) seems adequate, but the illustrations given to demonstrate how a command ought to be implemented (also *content*) do not seem adequate, you may wish to work further on implementation at home. If the *content* of a message seems poorly *organized* so that the sermon has more than one *purpose,* you may wish to sort the discrete pieces of *content* and rearrange them on your own so that they form more logically consistent wholes that you can readily use in your life. And, so it goes.

Understanding various parts of a sermon helps you to distinguish the desirable from the necessary. Take *delivery,* for instance. Your preacher stands stiffly in the pulpit and uses no gestures. He also speaks so softly that much of what he says cannot be heard past the tenth pew. Though it is highly desirable for a preacher to be animated when speaking, gestures are not absolutely essential. After all, you listen to perfectly intelligible radio preachers whom you cannot see. But if the preacher cannot be heard, that is a matter of a different order. The problem *must* be solved. One way is to start a fund for a P.A. system by giving the first gift (substantial, if possible). Be sure, however, in doing so, that you go through the elders in an orderly manner. Explain that you want to help rather than criticize and that you are anxious to solve the hearing problem.

Some items are borderline. For instance, you may be able personally to take abstract teaching and transform it into life by applying it to concrete situations. If you can do this, you are probably already a good listener. But, you know your teenagers can't and are having a problem with preaching that never applies, never illustrates, never implements. What should you do?

Well, perhaps one way of correcting the problem may be to ask the preacher—more than once may be necessary—"Can you give me an example or two of how the principle you taught us last Sunday can be applied to life?" If he comes up with a good response, thank him and tell him how helpful that application is. Suggest that perhaps it would benefit others as well as you if he could include more of that sort of thing in his messages regularly.

If he comes up with little or nothing in response to your question, you might explain that if it is difficult for him to apply his teaching on the spot, after studying it in depth, it's even more difficult for teens and their parents to do so when they hear the teaching for the first time. You might suggest it would be very helpful for him to take time to include such material from now on. Be kind, but make the point that if he can't immediately apply his teaching to life, he certainly shouldn't expect his congregation to do so. Any preacher worth his salt will take such words to heart.

Organization, when good, helps you think through *content* in an orderly way that leads to certain conclusions. Some preachers organize poorly. *Content* that should be reserved till later is introduced too soon and other material is not introduced soon enough. Take it down in the order in which it is given. Then, at home put the *content* into a more logical order. This is a great way not only to review, but also to think through what was said. When you put effort into studying the sermon, you reinforce what you heard and make it "your own." It becomes more a part of your own convictions when you have processed it yourself.

Interpretative questions may call for further discussion or commentary work. Remember, not all commentators agree, and surely you will not always agree with your pastor. Don't make a big deal out of occasional disagreements about the meaning of a passage. It is only when you find yourself regularly in disagreement over, say, a period of six months, that you should do something about it. If good commentaries always agree with your pastor, you'd better think through your own principles and methods of interpretation. Perhaps you need to ask the pastor for help. If it is the other way around, however, perhaps you ought to start buying your preacher some of these commentaries as Christmas and birthday gifts. As a last resort, after all else fails, you'd better have a kindly chat with him about the problem.

Coping with Purpose Problems

Because it is fundamental, I want to say a word more about *purpose*. I have suggested earlier that you summarize the sermon into a crisp, personalized purpose statement: "God wants me to forgive those who repent of wrongs done to me." Many preachers, however, were poorly taught about this matter, leading to several major problems and many minor ones. Three significant problems are:

1. The sermon may have multiple purposes, rather than one.
2. The preacher's purpose may be other than the purpose for which the passage was given.
3. The sermon may have *no* purpose.

Let's dispose of the third problem first. Many preachers were taught to look for the "central idea" or the "thesis," or the "big idea" of their preaching portion of Scripture. They might be able, therefore, to give you a thesis statement or central thought that summarizes the meaning of the passage, but were you to ask them the purpose of the message, they might stare blankly at you. Baffled, some might say, "My purpose is to preach a sermon; after all, that's what they pay me to do every week." Ideas like this, expressed or not, may be the only purpose such preachers know anything about.

To see nothing more than this in a passage is to begin preaching with no clear destination in view. Those preachers who aim at nothing can be sure to hit it. Every sermon should go beyond a literary analysis, in which the main idea of a passage is discovered. Preachers who do not preach with a clear purpose in mind for the congregation, usually end up discussing the "meaning" or "teaching" of the passage, and perhaps (if there is enough time—tack on some kind of application at the end.)

God did not give us the Bible merely to analyze and discuss; He is dissatisfied when we stop with knowing "the meaning of a passage." Which leads us to the second problem: the preacher's purpose (assuming he has one) differs from the purpose of the preaching portion of Scripture.

Purpose goes beyond meaning. It is one thing to say, "I understand what the words in a passage of Scripture *mean*." It is quite another to say, "I know from this passage what change in my thinking, belief and/or actions the Holy Spirit intends me to make."

Because they have never been taught that the object of their studies is to discover the Holy Spirit's purpose and because of a long tradition of using passages for the preacher's purpose(s), many sermons are less than adequate. Preachers should use preaching portions of the Bible for the purpose(s) for which they were given.

Since many preachers are only now beginning to become aware of this vital fact, you may have some work to do in this area. First, let's be clear about one thing: many otherwise helpful sermons—true to the general teaching of the Bible—have been preached from the wrong texts. When that happens, you may turn the failure into a double benefit. You may profit from the truths taught, and may even wish to search for a passage in which the sermon's purpose *is* found. That would be a useful study to make. In addition, it would be very profitable, if by reading commentaries, subsequent to the sermon, you could discover the Holy Spirit's purpose.

Finally, the problem you may encounter is that you may end up with more than one purpose statement since preachers who do not search out the Holy Spirit's purpose often "use" preaching portions for several purposes, sometimes called "lessons," of their own. Your task in such situations is to decide which, if any, of the purpose statements you formulated from the message is the one that truly expresses the purpose of the passage. If none do, then (again) you should make it your goal to articulate that purpose on your own.

I have said what I said in this chapter not to make you

more critical of preaching in the negative sense of that term, but to help you appreciate how difficult it is to preach well. So many things can go wrong! I also want you to better understand the "mechanics" of preaching so that you may make better use of what you hear.

One day a woman told Alexander Whyte, "I did not like your sermon!" But, that same week, her son had written to Dr. Whyte, "That sermon led me to Christ."[1] The sermon may or may not have been good—technically—but the Spirit of God used it mightily. Remember, while every listener is obligated to listen as faithfully as possible, how the Holy Spirit uses His Word communicated and received by our feeble efforts is His business. He is not limited by our weaknesses! Be grateful that He is always better to us that we are to one another!

CHAPTER FIFTEEN
Conclusion

So far as I know, this is the only book that tells you how to listen to a sermon. I hope, therefore, I have adequately covered at least the principal areas that should be of concern to the average listener. If there are what seem to you to be glaring omissions, I would be anxious to learn about them, and quite willing to consider them for inclusion in a future edition. Please write to me in care of the publisher.

In summary, consider this statement by Karl Heim:

> And Jesus says that God and His Word, which alone can supply meaning to our lives, can be approached only by those who are willing to make a complete surrender, who come with the fervent wish to be filled entirely by Him. If we come in any other way—as, say with a desire to be entertained—then our church attendance, our hearing of the Word and our reception of the Lord's Supper are an insurrection against God. It would be far better if we remained outside. Christ will spue us from His mouth as a man would lukewarm water.[1]

Strong words, but true! God bids you approach Him and His Word as active, receptive, eager, prayerful listeners. Slouching attenders, lazy in body and mind, may expect no blessing from Him. Physical presence, in and of itself, means nothing; indeed, as Heim says, it may be viewed as "insurrection," rebellion against God. We must rather learn to "sit with energy," as someone put it—energy supplied by the Spirit and focused according to His Word. In too many churches the cross, has been replaced by the padded pew.

The poorest evangelical preacher offers you infinitely more that the "teaching servant" in a Jehovah's Witnesses' Kingdom Hall, or a bishop in a Mormon temple. Wake up to your privileges. Be thankful. Take advantage of your blessings!

How tragic it is when believers show more concern on Saturday night about what to wear to church than they do about preparing their hearts to receive God's message.

> Some people . . . never listen to *what* is being said since they are interested in only what might be called the gentle inward massage that the *sound* of words gives them. Just as cats and dogs like to be stroked, so do some human beings like to be verbally stroked.[2]

That must never be the Christian approach to preaching. Christians must get deeply involved in sermon *con*tent, never con*tent* until, like the Bereans, they have verified its truth from the Bible. The Christian listener grows by the teaching he receives and the effort he expends to understand and evaluate it.

Moreover, he is one who puts his knowledge to work for the benefit of others. He grows from listening to preaching because he turns truth into life and ministry. He revels in change and expects each sermon to bring about changes in him that will make him more pleasing to God and more able to love others.

Your goal, therefore, should be to become an expert hearer; one who listens as God wants him to.

Two sons were asked to work in their father's vineyard. One readily agreed, the other refused. But, the one who agreed, didn't do the work; the son who refused, repented and did the work. Jesus makes the point that God would rather have obedience than talk. Has your seeming eagerness to attend the preaching of the Word been little more than an appearance for appearance's sake? Have you been like the son in the vineyard saying, "Yes, Father, I'll gladly go," when (with good intentions or not) you fail to follow through? Has sermon consumption yielded little change in your life or ministry?

If so, repent and take heart. No matter how late in life your resolve may come, you can still exemplify the obedient son. Clearly, the parable also teaches that God gives His children another chance!

Perhaps you've been struggling for some time with problems associated with getting the most out of preaching, trying this and trying that. You've become increasingly discouraged. Now, having read this book, you see light in the forest. Take it to heart. Don't put off what you can begin *this* week! In God's plan, preaching takes place every week. That means you can begin right away. Make this Sunday, and its sermon, an incredibly worthwhile experience—the first of many!

CHAPTER SIXTEEN
Sermon Slices

In the pages that follow I have provided thirty-one "slices" or excerpts of sermons—one for you to work through each day for a month. These slices are from sermons that were actually preached. In them you will find poor preaching and good. Interesting preaching and dull. New ideas and old. Truth and error (even heresy). You will want to approach them in the proper frame of mind—as a Berean looking for truth from God that will change your life. Don't search for error; let it crop up as you encounter it. Remember, even then, you may learn some truth *by contrast.*

These sermon slices are provided for you as samples on which you may practice some of the principles you learned in this book. I suggest that you read each excerpt through *once,* jotting down as you read any seemingly significant, new, helpful, questionable, or heretical idea or sentence. At the conclusion of *one* reading, sum up the purpose of the sermon excerpt as you see it in your *Results of Studies* loose-leaf notebook. (You don't get an opportunity to go back and relisten to a sermon as it is being preached. Of course, you can do so later, if it was taped.) Then, put your work away for a while. At this point don't reread the slice.

Later, return to your notes and, using a concordance, Bible dictionary, commentaries, and cross-reference Bible, make a fuller study of the concept(s) you have noted. Compare (or contrast) what the Bible teaches elsewhere, allowing Scripture to interpret Scripture. At the end of this study (which you may find will spread over more than one day), write out any conclusions you may have reached. Be sure to ask and answer the following four questions: 1) *How does God want me to change?* 2) *What must I do to implement the change?* 3) *What is the first step?* and 4) *When and where should I begin?* Then, put the results of your study to work in your life!

The sermon slices have all been excerpted from the sermons of preachers who are now dead and whose books are in the public domain. I have cited no sources in order to eliminate any preliminary bias for or against the preacher. Once you have completed your notebook, you may wish to compare notes with others who may also be studying these sermon slices. But be sure to do your own work the first time through these sermons, approaching them as you would when listening to sermons preached in your church. May you profit greatly from these studies.

O N E

Despair and denial are still twin brothers. Faithlessness and failure always go hand in hand. No man will dare and suffer for a cause which he believes is a doomed and discredited cause. No man will fight for a Christianity which he regards as "played out," or toil and suffer for a Christ who has "had His day." A man's enthusiasm for a cause is always in exact proportion to his faith in it. It is a lesson we need to remember in these days. For voices are loudly telling us that while Christianity has served the world well in past centuries, perhaps we need a different kind of religion in these days of ours; and that while Christianity is all right for us here in the West, Buddhism and Confucianism suit them better in the East. Now, once such talk is listened to, then good-bye to earnestness and courage and zeal. Let men believe that possibly a better religion may arise than the Christian, and the world will never see another martyr. Let men believe that Buddhism and Confucianism are as good as Christianity, and the world will never see missionaries like John Williams and James Chalmers, willing to lay down their lives in the preaching of the Gospel; or like Griffith John, willing, as he said, to labour for aeons and aeons if only he might save a soul. And perhaps that is one cause of our present-day weakness. We are paralyzed by our doubts and crippled by our fears. We are not quite sure of our Christ. We are not sure that Christianity is the absolute and final religion. We are not quite sure that Christ's is the only name. And so we risk nothing, venture nothing, dare nothing for our Lord and His cause. We are not sure that both may not be coming to an end. For our revival and prosperity it is a quickening of faith that we want, an unwavering faith in Christ, an unhesitating faith in our holy religion—that it is not a passing and transient thing, but the absolute, final abiding religion. According to our faith it shall be unto us.

T W O

But what have his sins to do with his palsy, the disease of his soul with the disease of his body? No doubt, his bodily pain and distress softened and humbled him, led him to examine himself and to repent. But more than this. In his sore affliction he recognized a certain connection between his disease and his sin. Therefore his own heart longed for deliverance from sin, while those who carried him to Christ only thought of the healing of his body.

Those who are at home in their Bible know well enough, that there is a deeply-rooted connection between sin and all manner of evil in this present world. "The wages of sin is death." This is the fundamental statement of the Scriptures furnishing the key to thousands of dark problems and mysterious facts in this world of wretchedness and suffering. Wherever in the life of nations, in the history of families, in the experience of individuals, sickness and distress, evil and suffering appear, there we hear the solemn voice of rebuke from the righteous and holy God: "Wherefore doth a living man complain? A man for the punishment of his sins? Let us search and try our ways, and turn again to the Lord. Let us lift up our hearts with our hands unto God in the heavens.

We have rebelled and have transgressed. Thou hast not pardoned." Thus the root and cause of all the misery of this world of sin is written in fiery letters, in the Word of the living God. Take away sin and that whole river of tears is dried up. But wherever sin remains its consequences continue. On many a human face and body the finger of God has written in legible characters the cause and origin of their particular disease. The prodigal son who had devoured his father's living with harlots, knew well enough the cause of his starvation and nakedness. When the drunkard's children go in rags, when his poor wife does not know where to find bread to satisfy their hunger, when he totters through the streets, a human wreck, unable to do solid honest work, we have, indeed, no difficulty in recognizing that divinely ordained nexus between sin and evil. When the young man who has ruined his health with carnal lust and lasciviousness languishes and withers in premature senility, a helpless and hopeless consumptive, we need not go far to seek the cause of all this wretchedness.

T H R E E

"One man shall die for the people, that the whole nation perish not!" What does all this mean, but that a raven, in spite of his rapacious nature, must bring the prophet his daily bread,—that all things, even the thorn in the flesh, even Satan's buffeting, must work together for good to them that love God,—that, if we are Christ's, all is ours, whether life or death, whether Cephas or Caiaphas?

How wonderful are the ways of God! How unsearchable His judgments! He makes the world that rejects Him work out His counsels, and fulfil all His purposes. Joseph in Egypt, having been sold by his brethren, saves innumerable lives from famine; Pharaoh cries to the messenger of God, in an imperious voice, "Take heed to thyself: see my face no more," and Moses solemnly answers, "Thou hast spoken

well, I will see thy face again no more;" Balaam, employed for
wages to curse the chosen people, must confess in spite of
himself, "I have received commandment to bless: and He
hath blessed, and I cannot reverse it;" David suffers himself
to be reproved by the cursing lips of his persecutor Shimei,
"Let him curse, the Lord hath bidden him;" a Herod full of
thoughts of murder and hypocrisy guides the wise men to
Bethlehem, saying, "Search diligently for the young child;"
the Pharisees in their very scorn have sung the song of songs
in praise of the Lord Jesus, "This Man receiveth sinners and
eateth with them;" in the name of constituted authority a
Pilate testifies the royalty of Jesus by the title on the cross:
"Jesus of Nazareth, King of the Jews," and likewise in the
name of humanity he preaches the sermon of sermons, the
greatness of which was unknown to himself.

F O U R

Are we capable of doing the same?—Does this question of
Judas concern us? *Is it I? Is it I?* Perhaps someone will at
once reply, "Thank God! It is impossible. Neither I nor any
poor brother of mine is capable of rushing into such a gulf. It
is effectually barred for us. Who is capable of betraying the
exalted Son of God? Who is able to sell Him who sits at the
right hand of His Father in heaven? What high priest would
choose to pay the money? Who will seize and bind Him who
has the keys of heaven and hell in His hands, who has all
power in heaven and earth?" Hush! Hush! There has never
been a sin, not even that which led to our Lord's passion, that
could not be committed again. The Christ above you, it is
true, cannot be delivered any more, but the Christ within
you, and the Christ that lives in the Church by the Word and
by confession. This question, *Is it I? Is it I?* Is of importance
this very day, even for you and me. Remember, in the first
place, that Jesus is your Master, and that you are His disciple.
You have walked along with Him. He has led you from infan-

cy. He has quickened you according to His Word and after
His loving-kindness. You have attended the Lord's Supper,
and have eaten bread with Him, yea, more than bread. At
your confirmation you have said, "Lord to whom shall we go?
Thou hast the words of eternal life. And we believe and are
sure that Thou art that Christ, the Son of the living God."
Nevertheless it is possible that you may become His betray-
er. Betrayal with you, too, begins in some solitary and dark
spot in the heart. One hidden spark, you know, can set on fire
a whole building. One small leak may sink a great ship. Disease in one part of the body may infect the whole, and end in
death. In like manner, a tainted spot in your soul may spread
ruin over your whole inner life, and cause you to be a betray-
er of Christ.

F I V E

Well, now, look back. See the way that you have come.
Recognise the leading hand of God. Your fathers served other
gods, and in this new land to which you have come, other
gods are worshipped, too. But our God, yours and mine, to
Whom we prayed in the wilderness, and Who hath given us
the victory, Who hath led us hitherto, to Him be all the glory
and all homage due. Not with your sword nor with your bow,
but by the mighty hand of God, has this new opportunity
been given to you. You are the chosen people. Choose therefore this day whom ye will serve in days to come.

Now I am aware that Israel's view of the nature of the God
of whom Joshua spoke was not quite ours. Let us look that
matter quietly in the face. It was not so lofty. The God of
Israel was a grim deity,—as Joshua describes Him in the
context of this chapter, a jealous God,—although we know
better now, because someone bearing the very name of Joshua—for Jesus is that name—came and told us about a Father
who loves and cares. But if Israel had never witnessed for the
God they thought they knew, we should never have been

here to worship the God that Jesus gave. I want you young men to understand that before we go any further. It was Israel's faithful witness, or the witness of Israel's faithful few, to a God of righteousness, however austere their conception of that God may have been, a God of righteousness, that has made possible your Christian God of love.

S I X

"For"—to proceed—"it is God that worketh in you both to will and to do."

What a revelation! What a thing to say! What a thing for any man to believe to be true about himself! What a magnificent life is the life of salvation! What grace! What glory! What surpassing blessedness! God! God Almighty! His very Self, and not another, working in us! Working immediately, and with His very own hands in us! Awake, thou that sleepest! "When I was a child, I spake as a child, I understood as a child, I thought as a child: but when I became a man, I put away childish things." Surely! Who would not? For what a workshop, what a laboratory, what a forge, what a crucible is the soul of man, and my soul! What living materials to be wrought upon, and what living tools to work with! And what a Workman enters my soul, goes up and down in my soul, takes all those tools and instruments into His hands, and turns them in upon my soul to its salvation! What a Master-Workman working in us, and we working in our own souls under Him! And our souls all the time the workmanship and the everlasting output of God, and of ourselves under God. That, then, is God! That is God, and no man ever told me! That is not chance, or accident, or mood of my own mind: that is not a man, or a man's book, or a minister's sermon acting on me! That is God with all those tools in His hands. That is God at His God-like work of making me to will and to do. Making me willing and able to pray, to repent, and to reform. Making me willing and able to think, to stop and consider, to open my eyes, to look behind and before, to take that right step, to enter my own soul and to see what still lies to be done by me in my own soul, to stand no more idle, to work while it is day, — seeing the night cometh when no man can work.

S E V E N

Seek the things that are above, where Christ is, and seek them through this Christ to Whom by faith ye are joined, "for ye died, and your life is hid with Christ in God."

Sometimes these words and others like them have been held to justify a form of other-worldliness which is not helpful nor admirable. There is hardly a text in Scripture which cannot be misconstrued and made to justify the light which is darkness. *Quot homines, tot sentenioe* — so many men, so many opinions. And almost every doctrine that has been preached in the name of Christianity, however vicious and shortlived, has been justified in some fashion from Scripture.

There has been a form of other-worldliness, perhaps it still exists, which is absolutely mischievous, and which has been justified from passages like this; it has taken the form described by Milton in that well-known phrase, "a fugitive and cloistered virtue." There is the absolutely selfish man who, in quest of the salvation of his own poor, petty soul, shuts out all consideration for his brother's needs. There is the man who cares not how the world goes so long as he is not made to suffer any inconvenience, and there are people of such sensitive and fine feeling, so called, that they cannot bear that there should be any jarring note in the music of their lives, or wail from the suffering world without. That is not the other-worldliness, you may be perfectly certain, of which St. Paul speaks. For this man, a prisoner of Jesus Christ, suffering stripes and bonds for His sake, toiling with his own hands that he might be free to carry the Gospel where he chose, this man, who was a missionary at a time when Christianity had been heard of only to be scorned, lived no easy life. When he said, "Seek those things which are above," he did not mean, "be indifferent to the things which are below."

E I G H T

Truth is always calm. It needs no defense. Error has forever been endeavoring to prove its own rights. Truth can afford to stand silent as did Christ before the great questioner asking Him "What is truth?" Error is clamorous. Truth is calm. This I prize greatly in Christianity. "Come and see," is its quiet, confident, open-doored invitation. There is no falter for credentials upon demand. But there is always a super-privilege for unquestioning faith. There is always an inner circle of experience for the faith which moves honestly and without the falter that waits on proof, upon the claims of our Master. "Reach hither thy finger, Thomas." Here are the nailprints. You shall not be disappointed even if you demand to put your hand into My torn side. I have not one single wound that is too precious to Me to be used to settle your troubled soul. But, Thomas, when you stand with your demanding fingers in the submitted scars, I will indeed be glad for you, and I shall count it high privilege even thus, under at least the colors of suspicion, to see you convinced! I want, however, to say to you thus won, and because you are won I can now speak over you a greater word than I could possibly say, had you not come along this limping way of a questioning approach, "Blessed are all those who have not seen and yet believed." Don't you see how much more to Me it means for them to believe Me, than it does for you to prove Me?

There is a sublime dignity about a genuine faith in God that scorns demanding proofs. "Except I see" is flavored with suspicion. It has never been a great leader. It has attempted no great campaigns. It has made no heroic sacrifices. It has been a mere recruit.

N I N E

Now it may seem that there is a somewhat abrupt transition here. The connection between the last phrase of the verse and what has gone before may at first sight be hardly apparent. Why, having spoken of "bearing fruit," should Christ turn straightway to the quite different matter of successful prayer? And yet, if we look deeper, we shall see that in thus speaking of prayer which attains its object Christ was really rounding off the process of thought which lay underneath the previous words, adding the last link in the chain of ideas He has been setting forth. In this way, "I chose you and appointed you"—I, who come from the Father and represent the Father, claim you. "That ye should go and bear fruit"—when you submit yourselves to My choosing and appointment, your life grows rich in the inspiration that flows from Mine, and becomes like Mine; and since My life is the Father's your life becomes like the Father's too. And then, as your life grows like to God's, the harmony of thought and feeling between you and Him will make you desire what He desires, and hope for what He will, and thus everything you request shall be given you. "Whatsoever ye shall ask of the Father in my name"—"in my name." When we have submitted ourselves perfectly to the authority of Christ so that His life beats through us, then we can never know an unanswered prayer or feel an unsatisfied want, because every prayer will be His own inspiration within us, and His inspiration is the inspiration of God Himself—so that the same God who answers the prayer is the God who inspires it also. When we ask anything in His name, anything that is suggested to our thought by our contact with Him, the prayer cannot fail.

Do you seize upon what I mean? It is not, I think, very hard to understand. "That whatsoever ye shall ask of the Father in my name, He may give it to you." It does not mean that God as it were makes a bargain with us: the power of obtaining what we want is not given to us in return for our recognition of and obedience to the Christ; but by recognizing and obeying Him our natures enter into similarity of sympathies with God's, and thus His aims and will are ours. When we bear fruit through submitting ourselves to Christ's choosing and appointment, our heart's desires will be such as God Himself has set within us.

T E N

For always, though Christ mixed with the morally fallen, He mixed with them not as One who sought to hide the measureless difference between Himself and them, but as One who pressed it home upon their apprehension by every action and every word and every tone: round about Him hung ceaselessly an air of spiritual uniqueness which He never permitted to be unseen. Indeed, it is one of the most marvellous testimonies to Christ's absolute separateness from the ranks of men, that He could thus walk upon the levels where the lowest lay, and yet keep quite unimpaired that impression of perfectness which ever proceeded forth from Him upon those He met. Your great man forfeits something of reverence if he stays too long and too familiarly at the side of those smaller than he. Christ, with the crowd of sinful ones thronging upon Him, preserved always—and meant to do so—that atmosphere of spiritual greatness which made it impossible for any one to touch even the hem of His garment except with awe. Whatever else He veiled from human sight, His spiritual grandeur, at any rate, He caused changelessly to pour its glory forth; and His method was ever to make sin, even while He dealt kindly with it, be thrilled with the contrast of the sinlessness He showed.

The soul that would attain to its best must not fear—must seek rather—to appreciate and dwell with the contrast of a perfect Christ. The more we realise how far separated from us He is, the nearer to us and the more powerfully upon us will His morally elevating ministries come. One of the most real reasons why the spiritual impulse obtains to-day so feeble a sway in the hearts of men lies, I believe, in this—that everything possible is said and reiterated again and again whereby the distance between common humanity and Christ can be made to appear less, and hardly ever a word emphasised whereby the contrast, which is really high as the heaven and broad as the earth and deep as the sea, between humanity and Christ would be forced upon human thought.

E L E V E N

But the point I want specially to make is this—that, under the conditions of life to-day, this turning back at the critical moment is not always an obvious and patent thing—that we may even in a manner turn away from the fuller significance of discipleship without knowing it—and that the need for self-examination is therefore all the greater. I have been saying that after the stage of being attracted by Christ's sweetness there has to come, and ought to come, the testing-hour when we see that there is something more than sweetness in Christ. But for some of us that testing-hour may have come and gone, and we may have failed beneath the test, and we may have left Christ to go without us on those higher, further paths where He called us to accompany Him—and we may not know it to this day! Then, when He walked our earth, when discipleship had something external about it, when allegiance to Christ meant an actual physical companionship—then a refusal to go the whole way of course announced itself at once. When the heart refused to go on, the feet retraced their steps or stopped short. But to-day the refusal of the heart is so easily disguised; and men and women who have really severed themselves from the Christ imagine that they are with Him still; and souls are complacently unconscious of the fast-growing distance between themselves and Him who has vainly called them to come over the further stretches of the disciple's way. There is no outward sign. Ah! to imagine that we are going on and on along the way in obedience to a

Christly leadership, while all the while Christ's larger revelations have really arrested and checked us, and we are faltering or going back—I believe that there is far more of that than we suspect, that this is, indeed, one of the most blighting curses that rests upon the Christianity of the day! People remain in contact with their own imagined conceptions of Christ, while they are really parted from Christ Himself; and they take their imagined conception for the reality, and grow enthusiastic about it, and I dare say get a certain amount of good from it (I am not going to say otherwise), and the warmth of emotion roused in them by the contemplation of it is held to be evidence of a whole-hearted consecration and of a discipleship that is ready to go all the way! I repeat—people remain in contact with their own imagined conception of Christ, while they are parted from Christ Himself!

T W E L V E

And there is nothing amiss in thus putting the emphasis on service. We must show our faith in our works. If we believe on Christ we must devote ourselves without reserve to His service. If the world is to be won for Christ every one who is Christ's friend must do his part. Nevertheless it is important that we keep ever in mind the truth that without faith it is impossible to please God, that we are justified by faith, that it is only through faith we are united to Christ and receive power for life and service. Abraham was simply to believe God—that was all. He had nothing whatever to do with the fulfillment of the promises. Nor have we. Faith links us to God, our littleness to His almightiness, and then He does the work—not He without us, certainly never we without Him, but He in us and through us. Let us get a fresh vision of the meaning and importance of faith. The sublimest measure of work without faith will accomplish nothing.

T H I R T E E N

We would better keep our hands off God's providences. Many a beautiful plan of His is spoiled by human meddling. Peter wanted to keep Jesus back from His cross. Suppose he had done so, what would have been the result? No doubt, many a time, love has kept a life back from hardship, sacrifice, and suffering, thereby blighting or marring a destiny, a plan of God. We are likely to pity the boy Joseph as we see him enter his period of humiliation, and as we read of his being sold as a slave, then cast into irons. But we see well that if human pity could have rescued him from this sad part of his life, the glorious part that followed, with all its blessed service to the world, would have been lost.

F O U R T E E N

Underneath the current lukewarmness in this matter—the underlying reason for our failure to apprehend the necessity of a real change—is this mistake. We have got into the way of measuring, as it were, the mere *quantity* of wrong things we have done; and so, of course, while the criminal and the evil-liver—the people who have run up a large arithmetical total of sins—must make an evident break with their past, must indeed die to what they have been, people of a more respectable order, those who have only just touched the brink of the muddy stream of sin and have never fallen headlong into its depths, need go through no such crisis of the soul. Some of us appear to require only a small change or adjustment of the moral nature, because the number of our actual transgressions works out to but a comparatively small result. And it is from that shallow and utterly futile method of estimating our moral position that we must escape, it we are going to understand these things at all. What needs to be remembered is this: There is always an inner process of character-formation going on, which is bound to be in the wrong direction if it be not definitely taken in hand and turned into the right direction: a man is always, however outward appearances may disguise the fact, getting either better or worse, not necessarily in the things he *does,* but in the thing he *is,* as regards the extent to which all the motives and preferences and loves and instincts of his inner nature are made of good; and until a man gives a positive impulse in the better direction to all these inner processes of his life, they will bend themselves toward the wrong. Movement, development, of some sort or other, in this realm of the inner moral constitution there must always be; and for every man, if he is to be a Christian man in the true signification of the word, there must come the moment when he decides that henceforth the movement shall be a movement toward good, the development a development of good. That *is* conversion—a check to the wrong development which has been going on within and an initiation of a better development in its place.

F I F T E E N

On the night of farewell Jesus trusted the power of memory, the ministry of reminiscence, as a mother does when she says good-bye to her boy who is going out to meet the dangers of the world. His entire demeanour had, as its background, the feeling that what He did would not be forgotten. Happy is he and safe who is armoured with holy memories in the dizzy hour of temptation, into whose heart comes the "touch of a vanished hand or the sound of a voice that is still," calling all that is best in the soul to stand fast. Peter remembered, and wept bitterly, to his cleansing; Judas forgot, and was lost—or else remembered too late, when sin had hardened into a dark and bitter despair that seeks solace in death. It is little we can do for each other in the deeper things of life, but we can so live in the home, in the temple of prayer, in the places of play, as to leave high and pure memories in the hearts of our fellows—like that sermon which I heard nineteen years ago, while a young student in Boston, which has lived in my heart every day, its thought still vivid, its very tones still eloquent across the years. The preacher never knew until I told him years later. Happy the man who in the susceptible, formative season of youth hears such voices of comfort and command, of inspiration and leadership; they are a possession forever. Not yet have we learned the meaning of memory—its depth, its power, its revelation, its ministry to the life of faith, for that it leads us back over the path we have journeyed and helps us to a clearer exegesis of the often strange medley of our lives. What a wonderful line is that of the Psalmist: "All the ends of the earth shall remember, and return to the Lord,"—as if at last the redemption of the race is to be a grand reminiscence!

S I X T E E N

All men admire cleverness, and the master commended the steward, not because he was unjust, but because of his shrewdness in using present advantage to make provision for the future.

Hence the strange saying of Jesus, "And I say unto you, Make to yourselves friends of the mammon of unrighteousness; that, when ye fail, they may receive you into the eternal tents." That is to say, Be as alert, as thrifty, as canny in the service of righteousness as men are in seeking their lower and unjust ends. It is a plea for practical acumen on the higher levels of moral effort, emphasising the importance of replacing futile and sentimental methods with moral sagacity and consecrated common sense. It is not the motive of worldly men that He approves, but their method, their strategy, their industry, their persistence, their wit in facing realities. He would consecrate sagacity, bringing the same shrewdness, which men use to win the prizes that perish, to the service of the life of the spirit. He urged that men should be as eager and insistent in behalf of eternal things as they are in the quest of earthly things—what Wordsworth called "the mystical side of good sense."

What He meant is best shown us in His own life. No one ever more completely divorced piety and stupidity, alike in His teaching and in the method of His labour. What richness of resource, what noble cunning in making lofty truth simple, what wise adaptability, what sweet strategy in winning the souls of men! Surely, if we may judge by His example, there is no reason why a sermon should be prosy or dull. Having the greatest of all stories to tell, He made use of every art at hand, employing the world as an infinite parable to illustrate His Gospel. Birds, flowers, the habits of the home and field, the weather, the games of boys and girls—with exquisite ingenuity He brought the simplest things to the service of the highest truth. He held that the sons of light must be wiser as well as nobler than the sons of darkness, if they would gain their ends. They must not only be courageous, but shrewd, and, above all, persistent, not content with ill-advised, timid, and intermittent efforts. There is hardly any lesson we need more to learn to-day, if we would be followers of One who was a great artist and a wise fisher of men.

S E V E N T E E N

The problem of the early Church was not a problem of the divinity of Christ but of the humanity of Christ; and that is the problem that has beset us in this present age. Again and again when I have been talking to people, and particularly to young people, about the problems of living, I have heard them say, "Well, you know, after all, Christ was altogether different from ourselves. It is true that we read that He 'was in all points tempted like as we are, yet without sin'; but because of His origin, because he was so unique, He was free from our human bias, and temptation did not mean precisely the same thing to Him that it means to you and to me." Now there could be no greater heresy than that. There could be no more fatal mistake in the thinking of individual believers than to imagine that Jesus of Nazareth was not a real man, facing real problems and taking real risks; and it is with reference to this aspect of Christ that we are now concerned.

EIGHTEEN

There was a day, to illustrate this point from ethics, when good people defended slavery from the Book, and were understood to make out a strong case. Certainly they did find many passages in their support, and made fine play with St. Paul's Epistle to Philemon. No Christian man now believes that a word can be said for slavery. No one now would be moved by a hundred texts in his favour. Slavery has been condemned both by the spirit and by the teaching of Jesus. When He taught the Fatherhood of God, the brotherhood of man followed, and the end of slavery became merely a matter of time. It is growing clearer that many doctrines of Christian men are not lasting, but that every word of Jesus is eternal.

NINETEEN

One of my fellow students went as a missionary to New Guinea, and he came back after some years of service. The last period of his service was in what is called the Fly River region, where James Chalmers, the great missionary, was murdered. When Chalmers was murdered, my friend went to take his place. He came back, and he came to see me. I had a long talk with him, and I said, "Tell me what you found at your station in New Guinea." "Found! I found something that looked more hopeless than if I had been sent into the jungle to a lot of tigers."

"What do you mean?"

"Why, those people were so degraded that they seemed utterly devoid of moral sense. They were worse than beasts.

If a mother were carrying her little baby, and the baby began to cry, she would throw it into the ditch and let it die. If a man saw his father break his leg, he would leave him upon the roadside to die. They had no compassion whatever. They did not know what it meant."

"Well, what did you do for people like that? Did you preach to them?"

"Preach! No, I lived!"

"Lived? How did you live?"

"When I saw a forsaken baby crying, I comforted it. When I saw a man with a broken leg, I mended it. When I saw people in distress, I took them in and pitied them. I took care of them. I lived that way. And those people began to come to me and say: 'What does this mean? What are you doing this for?' Then I had my chance and I preached the Gospel."

"Did you succeed?"

"When I left, I left a church."

You cannot understand the Father, you cannot belong to the Father unless you get the Saviour heart.

T W E N T Y

Let us remember the words of Christ: "Whatsoever ye would that men should do unto you, even so do ye also unto them." Be just.

There is a very common mistake about the meaning of the precept. It is sometimes taken as though it required us to rule our conduct towards other men by their wishes; to do this would often be a folly and a sin. It really requires us to rule our conduct towards others by what our wishes would be if we were in their place; and this is a very different matter. In other words, we are to make what we see are their real interests our own. I have heard of a foolish father who, when one of his girls was fourteen or fifteen years old, gave her the choice of a pony or of remaining another year or two at school. The child naturally elected to have the pony, and most children of her age would do the same. The father's conduct was ruled by the child's wishes, and he inflicted on her a grave injustice. From what I remember of him I believe that he knew no better. A sensible father will not always act according to the wishes of his children, but will consider how those wishes would be modified and corrected if the children had a larger knowledge and a larger experience of human life. No wise man would wish to enjoy temporary pleasure at the cost of lasting injury. We are unjust to our children if we do not give them the benefit of our wisdom as well as of our love. And we are unjust if we do not, in applying this rule of conduct, give to other men who may be excited by passion, by hope, or by fear, the benefit of our calmer judgment; and if we do not in all cases guide our conduct towards them by what we may be sure is our clearer perception of their true interest, even when this requires us to act in direct opposition to their most earnest wishes.

T W E N T Y - O N E

One cannot yield to the force of Jesus' teaching on character without facing its last application and asking, Will the final Assize be held on faith or character? As a matter of fact, the best public mind under all religions has judged by character, and has done so with a keen sense of justice and a conviction of paramount authority. When the individual has to form an estimate of his neighbor in critical circumstances he ignores his opinions and weighs his virtues. No one, for instance, would leave his wife and children to the care of a trustee because he happened to be a Trinitarian, but only because his friend was a true man before God. It is a working principle of life that judgment goes by character, and if in the end it should go by faith it might be in keeping with some higher justice we know not here; but it would cover our moral sense with confusion and add another to the unintentional wrongs men have endured, in this world, at their fellows' hands. It were useless to argue about a matter of which we know nothing, and where speculation is vain. We must simply accept the words of Jesus, and it is an unspeakable relief to find our Master crowning His teaching on character with the scene of the Last Judgment. The prophecy of conscience will not be put to shame, nor the continuity of this life be broken. When the parabolic form is reduced and the accidental details laid aside, it remains that the Book of Judgment is the Sermon on the Mount, and that each soul is tried by its likeness to the Judge Himself. Jesus has prepared the world for a startling surprise, but it will not be the contradiction of our present moral experience: it will be the revelation of our present hidden character.

T W E N T Y - T W O

With a soul that is imperfect, discipline would simply be development. With a soul that is sinful, discipline must begin with deliverance. Jesus, as the Physician of the soul, had not merely to do with growth: He had to deal with deformity; and Jesus, who alone has analysed sin, has alone prescribed its cure. Before Jesus, people tried to put away sin by the sacrifice of bulls and goats, and so exposed themselves to the merciless satire of the Prophets; since Jesus, people have imagined that they could be loosed from their sins by the dramatic spectacle of Jesus' death, and so have made the Crucifixion of none effect. If sin be a principle in a man's life, then it is evident that it cannot be affected by the most pathetic act in history exhibited from without; it must be met by an opposite principle working from within. If sin be selfishness, as Jesus taught, then it can only be overcome by the introduction of a spirit of self-renunciation. Jesus did not denounce sin: negative religion is always impotent. He replaced sin by virtue, which is a silent revolution. As the light enters, the darkness departs, and as soon as one renounced himself, he had ceased from sin.

TWENTY-THREE

For primitive man, terrorized by a physical universe that he did not understand, God was usually an enemy. The wild beast that roamed the forests and ever and anon fell upon some hapless human to devour him was a god. The mighty river that overran its banks and swept away his crude possessions or blocked his flight from other approaching dangers was also a god. The thunder that roared when the lightning had cleaved the skies, the great trees that shook themselves as the wind moaned through their branches, the majestic orb of day that glided across the vast expanse of heaven's blue, the moon that wandered through the stars, and the twinkling stars themselves—all of these were gods to be feared and placated if possible.

And yet perhaps the word god ought not to be applied to these things, so utterly fearful to primitive races. They were more demons than gods, so long as they were only feared; and the placating of them was more of magic than of worship. But the idea of God as an enemy of man has had a persistent existence in human thinking. We find it almost dominating the Old Testament when reference is made to persons outside the chosen people of Jehovah. And even as late as the time of Colonial America we hear an echo of it as Jonathan Edwards thunders out his sermon of "Sinners in the Hand of an Angry God." The hostility of God to sin and evil without enmity to weak and sinful human creatures has been a conception hard for the mind of man to grasp. Alas, the God described today to little children is still sometimes an enemy to be feared!

But like a sunbeam struggling to penetrate a gloomy windowpane, there came even to early man a vague thought of God as friend—a capricious friend perhaps, but still a friend. In Egypt, the cradle of civilization, men noted that the river Nile made possible their livelihood. They deified the friendly Nile. In other lands still other natural objects of size or power, too great for early understanding, came to be worshiped as friendly deities. *Real religion began when men first conceived of drawing near a superhuman power that might be friendly to their needs.*

In the Old Testament we find that Abraham was the friend of God, and after him Jehovah, still the enemy of less fortunate peoples, was the friend of the children of Abraham.

TWENTY-FOUR

So it seems that these little lives of ours are not so little and unimportant as we think. We project the shadows of ourselves out upon the world, and we throw them upward into heaven itself. We think we play our part on a very narrow stage, and to a scanty audience, sometimes to no audience at all—there is simply the monologue of our thoughts, of good or ill. But it is not so. We are all the time playing in the open, before an invisible audience, which is silent indeed, but intensely critical; by whom our acts are weighed, and our words, the very lightest of them, remembered. Indeed, we speak no word, even in a whisper, but it strikes upon the deep skies overhead, and the skies send it on reverberating over into the eternities. True it is, God knows us, every one of us—knows us as others cannot know us, and as we cannot know ourselves. We are all the time making new records, and Heaven keeps them safe; as we shall know some day when the books are opened. What others may think of us may not matter much; but it does matter what Heaven thinks of us, what these unerring registers say of us. Perhaps none of us would like to hear the record now, just as it stands; at least, not before our sins and failures have been forgiven and forgotten.

T W E N T Y - F I V E

The other great Christian principle is that, in all personal relationships between men and women, sex is sacramental. By "sacramental" I mean this: that that physical something which marks off the relationships between man and woman from those between man and man or woman and woman is never, ideally, *merely* physical or sensuous, but always a symbol, a token, an expression of a deeper moral and spiritual relationship. This view of sex contact is inherent in Christian thinking which, with Christ, sees all the visible world as the expression of infinite mind, and man's body as the expression of man's soul. On this view love means a spiritual union, of which marriage is the supreme sacrament. Here, at its highest and noblest, is "the instinct to create, going forth in the power of love, proving to us day by day that only love can create, bringing us nearer to the Divine power, who is Love, and who created the heaven and the earth." Any physical passion which is enjoyed as an end in itself, and is no sacrament of true love, is a revolting and degrading thing, akin to—indeed lower than—the intercourse of animals.

T W E N T Y - S I X

Dr. Dale and Archbishop Trench received a severe rebuke from the official organ of the Society because they ventured to take part in the Tercentenary Shakespeare Celebrations at Stratford church. They were accused, in the sonorous language of the day, of "trailing their Christian priesthood in the dust by offering homage at the shrine of a dead playwright!"

Now it ought to be recognized that this attitude of complete disapproval of all amusements, however strange it may seem to us, was in fact the expression of a natural and vigorous reaction against the coarseness and sensuality of many of the amusements of that day. It was, as Puritanism has always been, a protest against the encroachments of godlessness on some of life's fair spaces. But it does unquestionably represent a maimed religion. There may indeed come times, as in a debased society, when the individual who would do right has no option but to break completely with human activities which, not necessarily wrong in themselves, have become, for him and his day, hopelessly entangled with evil. Then there is nothing for it, as Christ said plainly, but to cut off the offending hand or pluck out the eye. But that, as He showed also, is a desperate remedy, and it means a maimed life. It is safe to say that in our own day, while there is much that is morally perilous and even indisputably evil in contemporary amusements, the general conditions are not such as to justify the Christian in regarding and treating amusements generally as outside the Kingdom of God. It is, moreover, a shallow and arbitrary judgment — one still too prevalent in some religious circles — which would identify "the world" with this or that particular amusement. "Love not the world nor the things that are in the world;" as Christians we want to obey that precept, but there is no short cut to obedience to be had by deciding that "the world" means the theatre, or going to dances, or attending race-meetings. Unfortunately "the world" cannot be thus labelled and disposed of; as many of us have learnt by now, "the world" is really an inner temper or attitude which gets up with us in the morning and lies down with us at night, and can express itself in all sorts of ways that have nothing whatever to do with amusements. Nor have we any right frankly to abandon fair tracts of God's world to the enemy. There are too many people who still cling to the timid and ancient superstition that the devil has all the best tunes! That contracting of life in the supposed interests of righteousness, that building of fences in the vain hope of shutting out sin and shutting in holiness, is an operation which will receive little encouragement from an honest study of the earthly life of Jesus Himself, with all its sanity, its freedom, its happy comradeship, its hatred of cant and its limitless belief in the possibilities of human goodness. We should surely be closer to *His* mind if we set ourselves to reclaim for the Kingdom of God everything human which is redeemable.

TWENTY-SEVEN

Two questions which harass the religious mind in our day were never anticipated by Jesus' hearers: they were impossible under His idea of Faith. When Faith is an isolated and subtle act of the soul, some will always ask, What Is Faith? and some will always reply, There are seven kinds, more or less, and the end will be hopeless confusion. If Faith be defined as the sense of the unseen which detects, recognises, loves, and trusts the goodness existing in numerous forms and persons in the world, and rises to its height in trusting Him who is its source and sum, then it is needless to inquire, 'What is Faith?' We are walking by Faith in one world every day with our souls, as we are walking by sight in another world with our bodies. No one asked Jesus, 'How can Faith be obtained?' because Jesus did not regard Faith as an arbitrary gift of the Almighty, or an occasional visitant to favoured persons, but as one of the senses of the soul. Jesus did not divide men into those who had Faith and those who had not, but into those who used the faculty, and those who refused to use it. He expected people to believe when He presented evidence, as you expect one to look if you show him a picture. One might have weak faith as one might have short sight: one might be faithless as one might be blind. That is beside the question. The Race has sight, although a few may be blind, and the Race has Faith, although a few may not believe.

TWENTY-EIGHT

It must be admitted that Jesus had moods, and in one of them He sometimes lost heart. One cannot forget the gloom of certain parables:—the doom of the fruitless tree; the execution of the wicked husbandman; the casting out of the unprofitable servant; the judgment on the uncharitable. He once doubted whether there would be faith at His coming; He prophesied woe to Capernaum; He wept over Jerusalem; He poured out His wrath on the Pharisees. But it was not about the world—the Samaritan woman, the mother from Tyre, the Roman centurion—His faith failed. It was about the Church—the Priests, the Scribes, the Pharisees, the Rulers. It remains for ever a solemn warning that while the Church is continually tempted to lose hope of the world, the one section of humanity of which Jesus despaired was the Church.

T W E N T Y - N I N E

In St. John's Gospel (12:20) we read of certain Greeks who had come up to the Passover Feast wishing to see Jesus. Schmiedel complains of the colorless way in which the scene is sketched. The two disciples, Philip and Andrew, seek to introduce the strangers; but what is the sequel? Whether the Greeks were admitted to see Him, what they said, what Jesus said to them—about all this we hear nothing. What follows in the record, it is suggested, is entirely irrelevant. But is it so? "And Jesus answereth them, saying, 'The hour is come, that the Son of man should be glorified. Verily, verily, I say unto you, Except a grain of wheat fall into the earth and die, it abideth by itself alone; but if it die, it beareth much fruit. He that loveth his life loseth it; and he that hateth his life in this world shall keep it unto life eternal' " (23–25). Here was a reply to the Greeks, a direct contradiction to the worldly egoistic philosophy with which these strangers were familiar, of which perhaps they were disciples. Through self-denial the greatest benefits were to accrue to the individual and the race. All that was vital to souls and society must arise out of renunciation, humiliation, sacrifice. He who weakly loves his soul, pampering and indulging it in animal pleasure and vanity, loses it. He who wisely hates his soul, repressing and denying its tendencies to earth and sin, preserves it to life eternal. Egotism is an ignoble and a fundamental heresy. Yet such was the creed of the Epicurean, the creed of the Sadduccee. The deepest witness of the human heart agrees with the teaching of our Lord; for however we may flatter those who do well to themselves, we hold their sordid spirit and life in contempt. The Oriental paints in his own fashion the selfish worldling, intent on material reward and temporal felicity, no great or generous purpose in his soul. "The wretched man who in this busy world does not practice devotion, only cooks weeds in a jewelled saucepan; or ploughs his fields with a golden plough, only to sow tares; or fences his land with a hedge after cutting down his camphor-trees, only to grow wild grain." He has renounced the really precious things for the comparatively worthless, and such characters, however big their barns or considerable their goods, are never objects of admiration; the instinctive homage of the heart is reserved for men of an altogether different type.

T H I R T Y

But we are still mastered by the spell of the ancient tradition. We can hardly think of a man as a saint unless he is very quiet, placid, and subdued; if there is a touch of melancholy in him we are better pleased. He must not be too strong; he must be a little pale; and must not have too much flesh on him. A man of another sort, with plenty of muscle in his arms and plenty of colour in his face; with a ringing voice, a broad chest, sound lungs, a vigorous pulse, and a firm step; with a healthy appetite and a good digestion; with a cheerful satisfaction in the pleasures of life, and a buoyancy of spirit that rises above most of its troubles; with an elasticity of temper that refuses to be chained to gloomy memories and to be vexed by common cares, that prefers the glad open sunshine to the shadows of solemn cloisters — such a man hardly satisfies us. Without knowing exactly why, we find it hard to think of a man like this as a saint. A keen delight in common work and common pleasures seems to most of us inconsistent with the great life of Faith and with unbroken communion with God.

The late Canon Mozley, who is better worth reading when he is wrong than most other men are when they are right, has said some very suggestive things on this subject in his essay on the late Dr. Arnold, of Rugby, and they illustrate rather strikingly the point on which I am insisting. He thinks that in what he describes as Arnold's "vigorous, youthful, eager, intense, lively, affectionate, hearty and powerful character," there was a certain deficiency; that there was not enough of sadness in it to touch our deeper sympathies. He says that we are sorry when our friends are unhappy, but that "we do not like them less, but more—yet, more, for being so"—a sentence which, I think, is not true without considerable qualifications. For everything depends on the cause and the quality of their unhappiness; there is a kind of discontent and fretfulness which repels and is likely to quench affection. A willful absorption in sad memories, an excessive anxiety about personal interests, a refusal to be happy, make cordiality of love and friendship almost impossible.

Canon Mozley goes on to say, "Arnold's character is too luscious, too joyous, too luxuriant, too brimful. . . . The colour is good, but the composition is too rich. Head full, heart full, eyes beaming, affections met, sunshine in the breast, all nature embracing him—here is too much glow of earthly mellowness, too much actual liquid in the light. The happy instinct is despotic in him; he cannot help it, but he is always happy, likes everything that he is doing so prodigiously—the tail is wagging, the bird whistles, the cricket chirps." This is a caricature, and there are lines in it which are not to be found in the original. Arnold's strenuous energy, both in work and play, was perhaps, his most remarkable quality, and the idea of energy is hardly suggested by describing his character as "luscious" and "luxuriant." But though a caricature, the sketch is sufficiently accurate to be recognised. I remember reading Arnold's Life thirty years ago, and I happened to be reading at the same time the Life of John Foster, which, in its way, was an equally interesting and remarkable biography. I turned from one book to the other, and the contrast between them heightened the effect of each. To pass from the secluded, cheerless, meditative life of Foster to the life of Arnold was like passing from a close, ill-ventilated, neglected room into which the sun never shines, and where the song of a bird is never heard, and the grace of a flower never seen, on to the hillside, with a fresh wind blowing, the sky full of sunlight, and a view stretching over miles of glorious country to the open sea.

T H I R T Y - O N E

Half a century ago many unwise persons thought that children ought always to be shown the reasons for everything that they were required to do. This pernicious theory has happily lost its temporary popularity. It is obvious that children who were brought up under its influence could never be disciplined to obedience. But the inevitable conditions of human life must have made it impossible to translate the theory into practice. There are many things that can hardly be explained to a baby in long clothes. Even a child of six will not find it easy to understand why it should be compelled to take offensive medicine, or why any limit should be placed upon its innocent pleasures in the vineries and strawberry beds. It is doubtful whether even a boy of nine or ten can be made to understand why he should learn the multiplication table or the Latin declensions. He has to do it first, and to discover the reason afterwards.

The same principle holds in relation to morals. If a child is not disciplined to truthfulness, industry, kindness, before he can see for himself the obligations of any of these virtues, the chances are that he will never see that lying, indolence, cruelty, are hateful vices. Compel him to be industrious, and he will discover for himself the obligations of industry; make it hard for him to lie, and he will discover for himself the obligations of truthfulness; use authority to accustom him to kindness, and he will discover for himself the wickedness of cruelty. In morals, practice comes before theory.

And so, if we obey Christ, His commandments will soon shine in their own light. "He that *followeth* Me shall not walk in darkness, but shall have the light of life." It is not by mere meditation that we come to see the real beauty and excellence of Christ's commandments; we must obey them before we see how beautiful and noble they are. We must actually *follow* Christ if we desire to have "the light of life;" if we decline to follow Him till the "light" comes we shall remain in darkness.

Notes

Chapter One: There Is a Problem

[1]Jay Adams, *Pulpit Speech* (Nutley: Presbyterian and Reformed Publishing Co., 1971); Jay Adams, *Studies in Preaching*, Vols. *I, II, III* (Nutley: Presbyterian and Reformed Publishing Co., 1976); Jay Adams, *Preaching with Purpose* (Grand Rapids: Zondervan, 1982); Jay Adams, *Essays on Biblical Preaching* (Grand Rapids: Zondervan, 1982); Jay Adams, *Truth Applied* (Grand Rapids: Zondervan, 1990).

[2]The most accurate translation of the verse is: "How can they believe Someone whom they have not heard?" indicating that in preaching, Christ is heard. See Ephesians 4:21. Preaching involves listening to Christ.

Chapter Two: Before You Begin

[1]I have treated this matter in depth in a book entitled, *The War Within* (Eugene, Ore.: Harvest House, 1989). This book tells you how to win the inner war between the Spirit and the flesh (the old ways), in which every Christian must participate in order to progress in his Christian life.

Chapter Three: Preparing for Preaching

[1]Paul Lee Tan, *Encyclopedia of 7,700 Illustrations* (Rockville: Assurance Publishers, 1984), p. 746.

[2]William Gibson, *The Year of Grace* (Edinburgh: Oliphant, Anderson & Ferrier, 1909), p. 88.

Chapter Four: Your Basic Attitude

[1]C.S. Lewis, *The Grand Miracle* (New York: Ballantine Books, 1970), p. 161.

Chapter Five: Expectations, Predisposition, and Spiritual State

[1]See Jay E. Adams, *Back to the Blackboard* (Phillipsburg: Presbyterian

and Reformed Publishing Co., 1982), pp. 57ff.

[2]I say "is likely to be ineffective" because the nature of preaching itself is calculated to call rebellious and doubting Christians to repentance and greater trust of God's promises. Therefore, while there is no assurance that it will happen, the sermon, for which you came unprepared, may be the very vehicle God uses to make you willing to hear His Word. Either way, however, your responsibility is to approach preaching with a heart of love for God and faith in His Word (Heb. 4:2). Chrysostom once complained about people "not heeding" what he was saying, and "giving no attention to" his words. Yet, he hoped to "win them over to a better state of mind" by the persistence of his "preaching" (Homily 3 on Genesis).

[3]The word can be translated "apt to teach" or "teachable." In view of the minimal nature of the other requirements in Titus and Timothy (the elder doesn't punch people with his fists, doesn't get drunk, has only one wife, etc.) "teachable" seems the more likely translation. At any rate, no one can teach others unless he, himself, is teachable. One of the fundamental requirements of a good teacher is that he is always anxious to learn.

[4]Of course, if you fear change or avoid it because of embarrassment (pride), you will find preaching boring because you will filter out all newness, settling for clichés, comfortable truths, etc. But, in such a case, it is *you*, not the preacher, who is a bore.

[5]F.W. Boreham, *Faces in the Fire* (New York: Abingdon, 1919), p. 22. As Chrysostom once said, "Just as hunger is a sign of bodily health, so, too, interest in listening to the divine sayings [is] . . . a sure pointer to spiritual well-being" (Homily 4 on Genesis).

[6]Lewis Anderson, *The Speaker and His Audience* (New York: Harper & Row, 1964), p. 161.

Chapter Six: Work at Getting the Message

[1]The solution is not always in finding answers—as important as that can be. Sometimes it is even more important to find the right questions.

[2]Lewis Anderson, *The Speaker and His Audience* (New York: Harper & Row, 1964, p. 156.

[3]In listening, as in other activities, it helps to understand at least a bit of what is happening. Last week, in Australia, I was watching Australian Rules Rugby on TV. When someone explained a few, basic rules of the game, that made all the difference; at once, the game became much more interesting. It would be useful to read at least one good book on preaching. I suggest, for a starter, Jay E. Adams, *Preaching with Purpose* (Grand Rapids: Zondervan, 1986).

[4]The worst case of disinterest is found in those who want preachers to scratch their itching ears (2 Tim. 4:3). Preachers may not only preach what is pleasant, or interesting; often, they must "rebuke" (2 Tim. 4:2)—sometimes "sharply" (Titus 1:13).

Chapter Seven: Understanding the Message

[1]For more about how to deal with sin in your life after conversion, see Jay Adams, *The War Within* (Eugene, Ore.: Harvest House, 1989).

[2]J.N. Lenker, ed., *Luther's Sermons,* Vol 8. (Grand Rapids: Baker, 1988), p. 306.

Chapter Eight: How to Handle Poor Preaching

[1]Paul Althaus, *The Theology of Martin Luther* (Philadelphia: Fortress Press, 1970), p. 40.

[2]Daniel D. Walker, *The Enemy in the Pew* (New York: Harper & Row, 1967), p. 79.

[3]Johannes Quasten and Walter Burghardt, eds., *St. Augustine on the Psalms* (Westminster: The Newman Press, 1961), p. 341.

[4]T.H. Pattison, *The Making of the Sermon* (Philadelphia: American Baptist Pub. Society, 1898), p. 356.

Chapter Nine: Berean Listening

[1]Johannes Quasten and Walter Burghardt, eds., *St. Augustine on the Psalms* (Westminster: The Newman Press, 1961), p. 248.

[2]See Jay E. Adams, *A Call to Discernment* (Eugene, Ore.: Harvest House, 1988).

[3]Quasten and Burghardt, *St. Augustine on the Psalms,* p. 117.

[4]Ibid., p. 74.

[5]Ibid., p. 157.

Chapter Ten: Distractions

[1]John Chrysostom quoted in Jay Adams, *Sermon Analysis* (Denver: Accent Books, 1986), p. 34.

[2]C.S. Lewis, *Screwtape Letters* (New York: Macmillan, 1962), p. 17.

[3]Carole Thomas, "Open Letters to Preachers," *Practice of Ministry in Canada,* vol. 6, no. 1, p. 10.

[4]Jonathan Lynn and Antony Jay, *Yes Prime Minister* (London: B.B.C. Books, 1989), p. 236.

[5]A.H. Harry Oussoren, "Up Front," *Practice of Ministry in Canada* (March 1989), p. 3.

Chapter Eleven: The Preacher and You

[1]John Chrysostom, *On Wealth and Poverty* (Crestwood, N.Y.: St. Vladimir's Seminary Press, 1984), pp. 99–100.

[2]T.H. Pattison, *The Making of the Sermon* (Philadelphia: American Baptist Pub. Society, 1898), p. 361.

[3]Karl Heim, *The Gospel of the Cross* (Grand Rapids: Zondervan, 1937), p. 103.

[4]For details on reconciliation through forgiveness, see Jay Adams, *From*

Forgiven to Forgiving (Wheaton: Victor Books, 1988).

[5]Thomas Horton, *The Potency of Prayer* (New Tappan, N.J.: Fleming H. Revell, 1928), p. 92.

[6]Johannes Quasten and Walter Burghardt, eds., *St. Augustine on the Psalms* (Westminster: The Newman Press, 1961), p. 62.

Chapter Twelve: Implementation
[1]The Greek *hear* can mean "obey," especially if it is followed by the genetive. When followed by an accusative, it may refer only to perception of sounds.

[2]Henry Ward Beecher, *Plymouth Pulpit.* IV. (New York: J.B. Ford Co., 1875), pp. 280–281.

Chapter Thirteen: God, Your Neighbor, and You
[1]See my book, *Self-Esteem, Self-Image, Self-Love in the Bible* (Eugene, Ore.: Harvest House, 1987).

Chapter Fourteen: Technical Matters
[1]Gerald Kennedy, *A Second Reader's Notebook* (New York: Harper & Row, 1959), p. 305.

Chapter Fifteen: Conclusion
[1]Karl Heim, *The Gospel of the Cross* (Grand Rapids: Zondervan, 1937), p. 103.

[2]S. I. Haikawa quoted in Gerald Kennedy, *A Reader's Notebook* (New York: Harper & Row, 1953), p. 288.